THE
WIIE MAE
OKLAHOMA

0 · 9 HRS. 9 MIN. 4 SEC. · AUG. 27. 1930
. 15 HRS. 51 MIN. · JUNE 23 TO JULY 1. 1931
8 HRS. 49 MIN. · JULY 15 TO JULY 22. 1933

18 MAY '98
KBUO

TO MARK

WITH LOVE ...

MAY MOST OF OUR
DAYS BE

CAVU —

Solo

Sincerely
Wiley Post

FROM

OKLAHOMA

TO ETERNITY:

....

THE LIFE OF

WILEY
POST

AND THE

WINNIE MAE

by Bob Burke

KENNY A. FRANKS
SERIES EDITOR

GINI MOORE CAMPBELL
ASSOCIATE EDITOR

OKLAHOMA HERITAGE ASSOCIATION

OKLAHOMA TRACKMAKER SERIES

Copyright ©1998 by Oklahoma Heritage
Association

Printed in the United States of America
ISBN 1-885596-07-3
Library of Congress Catalog Number 97-69054
Designed by Carol Haralson

Page one: Wiley Post. Page six: Post and Harold
Gatty honored with a ticker-tape parade on July
2, 1931 in New York City. Courtesy *The Daily
Oklahoman.*

OKLAHOMA HERITAGE ASSOCIATION
201 NORTHWEST FOURTEENTH STREET
OKLAHOMA CITY, OKLAHOMA 73103

ON THIS SITE
WILEY·POST
LANDED·THE·"WINNIE·MAE"
COMPLETING·THE·FIRST·SOLO
FLIGHT·AROUND·THE·WORLD
IN·7·DAYS·18·HOURS·49½·MINUTES
STARTED·JULY·15·1933
RETURNED·JULY·22·1933

Dedicated to the memory of

F R A N K   P H I L L I P S ,

Oklahoma oil pioneer, who gave Wiley Post

the chance to fly the Winnie Mae into the

stratosphere and discover the jet stream;

and to Phillips Petroleum Company for

providing funding for this project and its

dedication in preserving the exciting history

of Oklahoma.

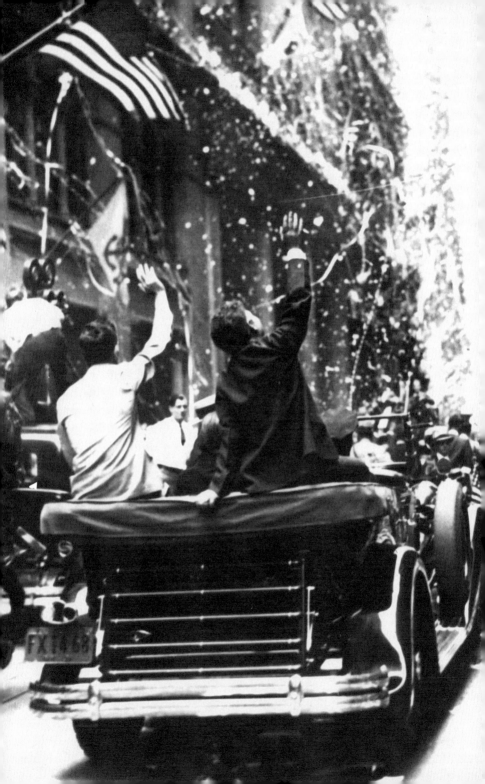

Acknowledgments

A MAN is only as big as the dream he dares to live. Wiley Post had big dreams. He died while yet young, but his dreams and his daring to live them out changed the pages of history for all mankind.

As a parachute jumper, test pilot, discoverer of the jet stream, inventor of the pressurized flight suit, and the first man to fly alone around the earth, Wiley gave his all to each of his life's endeavors.

I first grasped the greatness of Wiley's exploits when I flew in modern jetliners in an around-the-world trip in 1986. I marveled at how a one-eyed pilot from Oklahoma, in a slow, single-engine airplane made mostly from plywood, could have flown around the earth alone a half-century before.

I am honored to tell the story of Wiley Post, World's Greatest Pilot. I am deeply grateful to my wife, Chimene, my biggest supporter, I love you; Debi Engles and Eric Dabney for their help in research and transcription of interviews; my best friend Terry Davidson, and longtime friend and pilot H.W. "Pete" Peters, for reviewing the manuscript; Joe Carter and his staff at the Will Rogers Memorial in Claremore, Oklahoma; Carol Campbell and Mary Phillips at *The Daily Oklahoman* archives, for providing access to their fabulous collection of photographs of Oklahoma history; Dr. Reba Collins, fellow author and Will Rogers expert; Chester Cowen, world-class photographer at the Oklahoma Historical Society, for incredible photographs; Kathy Triebel, corporate archivist for Phillips Petroleum Company; and my son, Robert, for letting me put off for a few months building him a promised deck in his backyard.

In addition, I would like to thank Bill Welge, Rodger Harris, Judith Michener, Bill Pitts, Joe Todd, Delbert Amen and Scott Dowell of the Oklahoma Historical Society; Kitty Pittman, Melecia Caruthers, Mary Hardin, Adrienne Abrams, and Marilyn Miller at the Oklahoma Department of Libraries; and my dear friends at the Oklahoma Heritage Association, Paul Lambert, Executive Director, Kenny Franks, my mentor and editor of this series, and Gini Moore Campbell, a blessing to any author.

BOB BURKE

Contents

Introduction
WILL ROGERS PRESENTS THE WORLD'S GREATEST PILOT

*Will Rogers introduced Wiley Post and Harold Gatty to a Claremore, Oklahoma,
audience on July 2, 1931, at the opening of a new airport. Post and Gatty had just
stunned the world by flying around the earth in eight days.*

We are gathered here at these bountiful tables to do honor to
two gentlemen who knew that the world was cockeyed, but wasn't
right sure it was round. It seems fitting that this gathering should
be in Claremore, Oklahoma. Air is these boys' means of transportation, and Claremore has furnished more air to the world
through one native son than was her share.

A man wrote a book one time called *Around the World in
Eighty Days* and it was read for years. Well, if these boys after going
around it in eight days want to write a book, it ought to be read as
long as prohibition will be discussed, which means forever.

The physical hardship of this trip will stand out above all others. These birds stayed awake over seven full days out of eight, in
fact they haven't had any sleep yet. There must be no worse torture
and misery in the world than to have to keep going, when it looks
and feels like you can't possibly hold your eyes open, and how
wide theirs had to be open? That's what you call a sustained effort.
Well this was about the sustainingest effort that was ever sustained. They carried no parachutes, or rubber life boats, they simply made it or *else*.

Mr. Post is an Oklahoman. He did live in Texas as a child, but even Texas children grow up. Post used to be on a cotton farm. It wasn't ambition that drove him to the air, it was the bo-weevil. If it hadn't been for the bo-weevil and a Republican administration he might have remained an underfed, overmortgaged farmer. So you got to quit knocking the Republicans. They really made this trip possible.

Wiley got his mechanical knowledge from working in a garage when people who had learned their chauffeuring on a cultivator and mule transferred their knowledge to their first Model T's. He had no ambition about going around the world but he could take a wrench and go round the bolts on a Ford rim in record time. A plane crashed near the garage one day and all that was left intact was the propeller. Wiley took it and put it on an old Model T, in place of the fan, and took and soloed in it. That's why away up in Siberia when the ship hit in the mud and tipped over on her nose, and did enough damage to have sent most pilots back on the train, why he just took a hammer and some bob wire and fixed it so it added ten miles more an hour. The old garage training came in handy.

He piloted the plane on the whole trip. He was raised on a Texas "norther" and weaned on an Oklahoma "cyclone," so a little fog looked like a clear day to him. After he had flown over 700 hours, the government, on account of what they thought was a physical affliction by the loss of one eye, didn't want to give him a license. Now they got men looking and offering a bonus to One-Eyed Pilots. You see, the eye that he lost saw the bad weather and the bad landing fields, this one just sees the good. He is a determined looking little rascal, and when he says quit, you can be sure there would be no more gas, or no more air.

WILL ROGERS

Prologue

Death on a Frozen Tundra

Red airplane, she blew up—

C L A I R   O K P E A H A

THE ENGINE of the sleek red airplane coughed and sputtered. A haunting roaring noise was followed by eerie silence. Clair Okpeaha, an Eskimo seal hunter, saw the plane dive through the dense fog into the shallow water of a small river. The impact was so severe that nearby Eskimos were splashed with water. The plane's fuselage was broken and one wing ripped off. There was a crunching sound as the plane tipped over on its back.

Okpeaha was terrified but cupped his hand to his mouth and shouted to the two men in the plane. There was no answer. Oklahoma's two most famous citizens, Will Rogers and Wiley Post, were dead. It was August 15, 1935.

Okpeaha knew he should go for help. He began running as fast as his legs would go. It took him hours to run 15 miles across rivers and around frozen lakes to the U.S. Department of Interior station at Point Barrow, Alaska. United States Signal Corps operator, Stanley R. Morgan, was on duty when he heard a clamor on the beach outside his post. The natives were gathered around Okpeaha who was physically exhausted, but managed to gasp out in broken English, "red airplane, she blew up."

With his breath back, Okpeaha described the crash of the airplane at his sealing camp. He told Sergeant Morgan that the plane had circled several times before landing to ask for directions to Point Barrow. He described the two men as, "one wearing rag on sore eye; other big man with boots." Morgan immediately recognized the description of Wiley Post and Will Rogers as newspapers carried daily accounts of their flight across the barren tundra of northern Alaska.

Frank Dougherty, a local government schoolteacher and "stringer" for United Press, and Sergeant Morgan put together a band of more than a dozen Eskimos and boarded an open whaleboat powered by a small gasoline engine. Dodging chunks of ice and fighting strong currents, it took the rescue party more than three hours to reach the crash scene. It was now the early morning hours of August 16.

The hearts of the rescuers surely missed a beat as they saw the tangled debris of the smashed plane in the semi-darkness of the Alaskan night. The natives had recovered Rogers' body and placed it in a down-filled sleeping bag found in the plane. The world's most famous humorist had been sitting in the back of the plane's cabin and was easily reached by the natives. Post was pinned by the massive motor against his seat. It took rescue workers almost an hour to remove his body from the plane. Death had been swift and merciful.[1]

For six decades there has been debate about the time of the crash. Clair Okpeaha and his family thought it occurred around 7:00 P.M. However, one of the rescuers noticed that Post's watch had stopped at 8:18 P.M., forever marking in eternity the exact time of the fateful crash. The bodies were secured in the bottom of a small boat and towed back to Point Barrow. There they were taken to the Presbyterian Mission Hospital, operated by Dr. Henry Greist and his wife Mollie, a nurse. Together they washed the bodies and prepared them for the long trip back to America. It took the medical people five hours to clean and prepare the bruised and broken bodies. Outside the hospital, members of the rescue team sat patiently, lamenting the loss, whispering reverently.

Sergeant Morgan sent a radio message to Seattle to tell the world about the tragedy:

> Plane, out of control, crashed nose on, tearing right wing off and nosing over, forcing engine back through body of plane. Both apparently killed instantly.

Reporters and editors in newsrooms around the world gasped as they read the dispatch from Point Barrow. Presses stopped as a tragic headline replaced other news of the day. The *New York Times* banner headline announced that the nation was shocked by the loss of two of its most popular men. When news reached Washington, D. C., debate stopped in the House and the Senate.

The Associated Press story was straight and to the point:

> Will Rogers, beloved humorist, and Wiley Post, master aviator, were crushed to death last night when a shiny new airplane motor faltered and became an engine of tragedy near the outpost of civilization.[2]

The *Los Angeles Times* published an "extra" edition with full details of the tragedy that struck the hearts of millions. Newspapers in London, Berlin, Lisbon, Hong Kong, and other major capitals of the world devoted their entire front pages to the tragedy.

World leaders and famous people everywhere interrupted their schedules to express their shock. President Franklin Roosevelt left the oval office and promptly sent a telegram to the Rogers and Post families. Legendary aviator Amelia Earhart told the world, "Wiley Post is gone. Lost to the world are his ability, his humor, his conquering spirit." War hero Captain Eddie Rickenbacker called Post's death "a serious blow to the science of flying that will slow up man's next great step forward in the conquest of the air."

In Post's hometown of Maysville, Oklahoma, the *Maysville News* dedicated its next weekly edition to the tragedy. A large photo of Post was captioned simply, "Wiley Post, the World's Greatest Aviator." Local poet Dorothy Willis lauded the dead hero:

But the wings he knew have crushed and he is gone
And a million saddened hearts send up their prayer;
Now he flies a ghost ship in the Great Beyond
God grant him a happy landing there.[3]

American aviation hero Charles Lindbergh received news of the crash while celebrating his son's birthday in Maine. He called a friend at Pan American Airways and arranged for the bodies to be transported home. Joe Crosson, a veteran bush pilot and chief pilot for Pacific-Alaskan Airways, flew the bodies in a sea plane from Point Barrow to Fairbanks, and then in a Pan American Lockheed to Boeing Field in Seattle. Pilot William Winston, in a Pan American DC-2, took over the sorrowful task of bringing America's heroes home.

Will Rogers' body was removed at Los Angeles. Then the DC–2 flew eastward to Oklahoma City with the remains of Wiley Post. When the plane lumbered onto the runway at the Municipal Airport, 8,000 people were on hand. Wiley Post had flown home to Oklahoma . . . for the last time.

NR105W

WINNIE M
OF OKLAHOMA

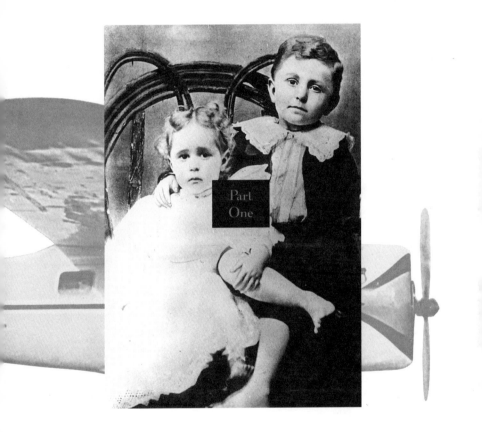

Part
One

A LIVELY BOY

Texas is a nice place if you are outdoors—

WILEY POST

ILEY HARDEMAN POST was born November 22, 1898, in his parents' modest farmhouse near Grand Saline, Texas. William Francis Post, a Scotchman and the son of a Texas Baptist preacher, married a pretty Irish girl, Mae Quinlan, and bought 160 acres of rich farmland in Van Zandt County, Texas, about 60 miles east of Dallas. William, Mae, and Wiley's three older brothers, James, Arthur, and Joseph, spent most of the year before Wiley's birth as itinerant farm workers in Oklahoma. On their way back to Texas, they stopped and helped bring in the crops at the William Hardeman farm near Denison, Texas. They liked Hardeman so much they chose his surname for Wiley's middle name.

When Wiley was three, Mae Post gave birth to a daughter, Mary. In 1902 the family bought 320 acres near Abilene, in west Texas, from a farmer who had "oil fever" and had left for Indian Territory and the lure of "black gold." Often the major topic at the Post dinner table was the discovery of oil in Indian Territory. Many of their Texas neighbors sold out and invested their life savings in oil leases.

With more land to farm came the need for machinery. Wiley was fascinated by machines and always remembered his first sight of a new harvester. His father had to escort the curious boy away from the sharp knives of the gleaming piece of new machinery.[4]

Wiley knew early in life that he wanted nothing to do with farming or formalized education. Wiley Post and school did not mix well. He started school near Abilene and his adverse reaction was obvious both to the teacher and to his parents. Wiley said, "Texas is a nice place if you are outdoors, but inside a schoohouse, under the thumb of a strict taskmaster, if you're six years old and having trouble with geography, it gets hot and dull."[5]

Another son, Byron, was born near Abilene before the Post family moved back to Oklahoma in 1907. Mr. Post found 160 acres six miles west of Rush Springs, Oklahoma. Three years later Post moved the growing family four miles south to the community of Burns. Wiley became more restless with his agrarian lifestyle and disliked school even more. He was upset that he was always compared to his eldest brother, Jim, the star student of the family. A classmate later recalled that Wiley was more interested in playing than learning and was "a lively, talkative and mischievous boy."

Wiley quit school at age 11, just as younger brother Gordon came along. Wiley thought he was "old enough to decide matters for himself."[6] He set out to prove his independence by earning money in the area "fixing things." He repaired sewing machines, household and farm machinery, and sharpened reaper knives. By the time he was 13, he had saved enough money to buy a bicycle, the only two-wheeled contraption for miles around.

The county fair in Lawton, Oklahoma, in 1913 made a major impact on the life of Wiley Post. There he saw his first airplane and car. Everyone around Grady County was talking about the fair and an "airplane ascent" that was to be part of the program that year. Wiley did extra chores around the farm to earn a few dollars to pay his admission to the fair. He was only 14, so Mr. Post sent elder brother Jim along in the horse and buggy to watch over him.

Jim and Wiley started out for Lawton late in the evening. It took all night for the buggy to travel the primitive, sandy 50-mile stretch from Burns to Lawton. Early in the morning they topped a hill and saw the fairgrounds. Wiley's curious and adventure-seeking mind raced as "the nag pricked up his ears and quickened his lagging steps."[7] The boys looked at the prize cows and pigs and the cotton and maize exhibits brought in by farmers in Comanche County. Wiley spotted displays of farm machinery across the midway. He and Jim started that way, but never made it. It was a moment that changed Wiley's, and the world's, history forever.

Standing out in the open field that served as the midway was a "queer-looking contraption." Wiley stopped. Before his "astonished vision," was an "aeroplane"—that's what they called them then. The county fair changed itself into an air meet for Wiley then and there. The machine was an old Curtiss Pusher. Wiley "promptly spent the morning with it." For the rest of his life Wiley declared that he had never seen "a bit of machinery for land, sea, or sky that has taken my breath away as did that old pusher."[8]

Wiley was in another world. He forgot to feed and water the horse that had been hitched to a tree at the side of the midway. He nearly got in trouble for hanging around the airplane. A constable chased him away at least ten times but he always returned, trying to get close enough to hear exhibition pilot Art Smith speak.

The show began as Smith showed off his Pusher with loops, spins and dives. He performed one of the earliest pyrotechnic displays by attaching roman candles to his airplane. Wiley's obsession with flying had begun.

When it began to grow dark Wiley sneaked back to the plane. He paced off its length and width and measured the height in "hands," just as he had seen his father and brothers step off horses in trades. He was sitting in the rickety seat—"they didn't have enclosed cockpits then"—when his brother found him. Wiley had promised to meet Jim at the spot where they had left the horse. However, Jim had been looking for Wiley for nearly two hours.[9]

Wiley and Jim headed for home with the horse and buggy. Wiley, the dreamer, had been secretly forming in his mind the Wiley Post Institute for Aeronautical Research. In fact, he was so engrossed in thought that, when he took his turn at driving the horse on that long night-drive home, he was imagining himself "doing the 30-miles-an-hour air speed of the Curtis Pusher."[10]

On the trip home Wiley got to ride in an automobile for the first time. "With much rattling and tooting," the car passed Wiley and Jim, nearly choking them with the heavy cloud of southwest Oklahoma grit. However, a few miles later, the boys came upon the car, mired in sand. The owner of the car tried to buy the Post's horse for a dollar, but Wiley had a better bargain. He would take the dollar, and a ride home in the car, in exchange for bringing help. About five miles down the road was Joe Crawford's sawmill. Wiley borrowed a team of horses and, with the help of several mill workers, coaxed the car to solid ground. Wiley climbed into the car and headed for the Post homestead. The machine age had begun, at least for 14-year-old Wiley Post.

The family gathered around the car as the owner replenished the radiator with water. The car trip from Lawton to the Post farm had taken far less time than with the horse and buggy. The machine and its speed amazed Wiley. He later said that trip seemed greater to him than even a flight around the world.[11]

Wiley used his new-found love for machines to help modernize the Post farming operation. He converted a gasoline engine water pump, by attaching a series of belts, to run a corn sheller, grindstone, buzz saw, and other handy, time-saving machines.

Wiley left home at 17. He disliked farming and could not stand the thought of going to school anymore. From age 11 to 17, his school attendance had been sporadic at best. The real world, and the need for money to live in it, forced Wiley to return home again. He made a deal with his father to make a cotton crop and share the profits. With that money he headed to Kansas City to attend a seven-month auto mechanic's course at the Sweeney Auto School. He graduated as a good chauffeur and mechanic, but still had a hankering for further knowledge along engineering lines.

He still thought about airplanes. No matter what he did or where he worked, he looked at each new piece of machinery "with the underlying thought that its principle might be applied to aviation." He read "a great deal," studied mathematics by himself, and experimented a bit with chemistry.[12]

In later years, brother Jim asked Wiley if he had ever intended to be an auto mechanic. Wiley told Jim he was going to "use" motors, not work on them.[13]

I'm In the Army Now

With a sharp jerk, the parachute opened—

WILEY POST

WILEY'S FIRST JOB away from the farm was as a driver and grader for the Chickasha and Lawton Construction Company, a firm contracted by the U.S. government to build an airport at Fort Sill. The airport was named Post Field, after Lieutenant Henry B. Post, who had been killed in California in 1914. He was no relation to Wiley.

Wiley spent many hours around the airfield, hoping to find some way to be accepted for flight training. America had entered World War I in April, 1917, and Wiley's three older brothers joined the Army. It also sounded like the right thing for Wiley.

In the summer of 1917, Wiley joined the Students' Army Training Camp on the University of Oklahoma campus in Norman. He studied radio, a course in communications that would prove incredibly valuable in his future career. Section A of the radio school graduated and was shipped overseas to France. However, by the time Wiley, in Section B, completed the course in 1918, the war was over, the Armistice signed, and Wiley discharged.

William Post had bought a new farm near Alex, in Grady County, in 1918 but Wiley had no desire to return to farming. Jobs were hard to find so he drifted to Walters, Oklahoma, where a new oil field was opening up.

He was well equipped to be a roughneck in the oil patch,

young and strong. His Scotch-Irish ancestry left him short, only five feet and five inches, but he was in good shape at 130 pounds. His training as an auto mechanic and his own experience of repairing things made him a handy employee around an oil rig. He made $7 a day as a roughneck, feeding boilers, climbing derricks to thread pulleys, all dirty and hard work. Soon he was promoted to tool-dresser and his pay jumped to $11 a day. There was no place to spend the earnings so Wiley saved a substantial sum. He, too, wanted to be an oil baron.

The gambling fever of the oil fields hit Wiley hard. He lost his first stake when he put it all into a wildcat scheme. He went back to work as a driller making $25 a day and soon saved another stake. But that disappeared also when he tried to "get rich quick by leasing ground near a wildcat well which petered out."[14]

Wiley's first airplane ride was a disappointment. In the summer of 1919 barnstorming pilots, who had learned to fly during the war, enchanted the citizens of small towns with acrobatics in their old planes held together with baling wire. Odie Faulk, in his biography of Clarence Page, another Oklahoma pioneer aviator, explained barnstorming:

> They tried to arrive at the town selected about 11:00 A.M., not doing any stunting but rather buzzing the main thoroughfare at a safe altitude of some 500 feet in order not to frighten horses. After some 10 minutes of this, by which time they could see people coming out into the street, they would land and wait. The two mechanics then would sell tickets for rides at five dollars each, making certain that passengers were strapped in safely. The three pilots did not do stunt flying, for they had learned that most passengers did not enjoy this; what their customers wanted was a safe takeoff, a flight around the town at several hundred feet, and then an easy landing.[15]

Wiley paid barnstormer Captain Zimmerman $25 for a ride in his open-cockpit biplane. When Wiley became "a little squeamish" in the air, he felt his ride was not the thrill he had expected. The plane was incapable of doing any startling stunt and Wiley felt that aviators did not necessarily have "those supernatural powers" he had been reading about in magazine stories.[16]

Unemployed and bored with life, Wiley turned to a less than honorable way to make a living in 1921. Sometime in the spring, Wiley began hijacking cars as they traveled around Ninnekah, a community near Chickasha. Wiley never talked publicly about the incident, but the events are recorded on page one of the *Chickasha Star*, the Grady County weekly newspaper, on April 2, 1921:

BANDIT CAPTURED AND LODGED IN JAIL

The hold-up man who has been causing so much trouble in Grady County was captured a few days ago by E.R. Mercer, S.A. McClain, Tom Wood and S.A. Null, all residents of the Ninnekah neighborhood. The man's name is Wiley Post and he was at once brought by his captors to the Grady County Jail. He stopped the automobile in which the four men were riding by placing an automobile casing in the road. When they stopped to investigate he stepped out and ordered them to throw up their hands but he soon found the tables turned on him.[17]

The police blotter signed by Wiley on the night of his arrest revealed a world of information about the single, 23-year-old suspect who faced the gloomiest night of his life. It contained his fingerprints, his parents' names and address in Maysville and a description of Wiley: "Medium build, 131 pounds, 5' 4¾", chestnut hair, scars on both arms, and droop shoulders." He listed his religion as "none," surely a disappointment to his Baptist parents. Wiley had 27 cents on him when arrested. He denied smoking, drinking or chewing and described his associates as "fair."[18]

On April 28, 1921, Wiley was convicted of robbery and sentenced to ten years in the State Reformatory at Granite. After he was incarcerated for only a few months, the prison physician, Dr. T. J. Nunnery, concluded that Wiley could not take prison life even though he was physically a perfect man and submissive and respectful as a prisoner. Wiley was paroled by Oklahoma Governor J. B. A. Robertson on June 3, 1922, because of his "mental condition."

The parole agreement referred to letters from Dr. Nunnery and Dr. George A. Waters that reported that Wiley was not given important duties to perform because he could not retain the order "long enough in his mind to perform it." His case was diagnosed as a "melancholic" state which, the doctors concluded, could not be improved by a change of duty or good treatment, and it was "steadily growing worse."[19]

Wiley agreed to the strict terms of the parole agreement on June 5, 1922, and was released, 13 months after entering the reformatory. He was required to file monthly written reports to the warden, was barred from drinking, gambling, or carrying firearms, and was ordered to "industriously follow some useful occupation, avoid all evil associations, improper places of amusement, all pool and billiard halls, obey the laws and in all respects conduct himself as an upright citizen."[20]

The robbery conviction followed Wiley for the next dozen years until he was granted a full pardon by Governor William H. "Alfalfa Bill" Murray on December 27, 1934. It has been said that when Wiley received the pardon in the mail, he could not look at it, but instead asked his wife to send it on to his parents as a small repayment of the misery and embarrassment he had caused them.

Wiley lived at home with his parents off and on in the early 1920s at their new farm just north of Maysville. It was not a pleasant, peaceful time of his life. So he went back to the rig and resumed his duties as a driller. "Seesawing between gambling the stake on a hole of his own" and working for other drillers, Wiley somehow was able to get through the next four-and-a-half years. Twice he thought he had "made the grade" by leasing ground supposed to cover oil, both times he was wrong. Then he got disgusted with the oil business. The price of oil went so low that none of the operators were anxious to drill.[21]

Wiley's persistent urge to fly came over him one day while

working on an oil rig near Holdenville. He saw a plane overhead and knew it was time to quit the oil business.

The area around Seminole, Holdenville, and Wewoka, Oklahoma, was booming because of a major oil discovery. The Greater Seminole Area was the world's chief producer of petroleum from 1923 to 1935. In 1923 the area was sparsely populated until news of the boom got out. When several large pools of oil were brought in in 1926, more than 100,000 people moved into the area within months. Hamlets and villages became cities overnight. The population of Seminole leaped from 1,000 to 30,000 in two months during 1926.[22] That congregation of people was good news for barnstorming pilots who could entice easy money from "rich" oilfield workers with parachute jumps, aerobatic maneuvers, and "penny per pound" plane rides.[23]

Wiley heard about a flying circus at Wewoka, Burrell Tibbs and his "Texas Topnotch Fliers." Wiley found the troupe and applied for a job. The only position open was "parachute jumper" because Pete Lewis, the exhibition jumper, had been injured in a landing the day before. Wiley turned on the charm and convinced Tibbs he could jump out of an airplane. With minimal training in skydiving, Tibbs directed Wiley to the back seat of the "worn and battered" Curtiss JN–4 airplane. When they reached 2,000 feet above "the usual rural airport Sunday crowd," Tibbs said, "OK. Get ready." Wiley's own recollection of the incident is priceless.

He was "somewhat taken aback," now that the time had arrived. He hesitated, "not so much through fear as through ignorance." He seemed to have forgotten all the things Lewis had told him to do. He looked back helplessly at Tibbs, but "got only a glare in return." Suddenly he recovered and threw one leg out over the wing. Tibbs cut his throttle so that "the slipstream of the propeller" would not blow him off.

"Let's go!" Tibbs shouted. Wiley "let go the strut and backed off the wing." He swung helplessly out underneath the wing until he remembered what to do next. Then he found the release string and pulled with all his might.

Suddenly all motion stopped. Wiley seemed to be floating. The plane was gone. With a sharp jerk, the parachute opened. He looked up and saw it spread out above him. "While still hanging tight to the ring," he first felt a sinking sensation. He swallowed hard and for the first time looked straight down. It was one of the biggest thrills of his life. The people below "looked like ants and the fields looked like brown or green carpets."

He watched the trees get bigger, "skimmed over the edge of a big sycamore which bordered a grove beyond the flying field," and lost the last few feet of altitude slowly because of the "cool eddies of air from the damp, plowed meadow beyond." There was only a slight bump as he flexed his knees for the landing. His feet stuck in the furrows. The wind took the parachute ahead of him, and he fell on his face.[24]

Wiley had successfully passed the first full-scale test of the Wiley Post Institute for Aeronautical Research.

A JOB WITH
THE FLYING CIRCUS

I was an actor, my own manager, and bookkeeper—

WILEY POST

WILEY SIGNED ON with the "Texas Topnotch Fliers" after his successful parachute jump. For what he did for free one week he was paid $50 the next. Soon he was making $100 for a single jump at a weekly airshow in some small Oklahoma town. He was assigned to the second airplane in Burrell Tibbs' flying circus and flew with a young pilot named "Tip" Schier. During the week, between air shows, Wiley received free flight instruction from the stunt pilots he worked with, especially a pilot named Sam Bartel. Wiley knew that someday he would be a pilot.

Wiley became famous as a jumper. He thought he could make more money on his own, so he said goodbye to Burrell Tibbs and began setting up his own air shows.

"Town boosting" was the order of the day in Oklahoma communities in 1924, so it was easy for Wiley to interest chambers of commerce and Rotary Club members in staging a parachute jump on Sundays. Frequently, he was paid as much as $200 for a single jump. He had to pay a pilot and lease a plane out of his price, but that seldom came to more than $25. He did not care how good or how poor a flyer the pilot was and always took the plane which was nearest the town in which he was to perform. He was an actor, his own manager, and bookkeeper, in addition to holding his place "at the head of the Wiley Post Institute."[25]

One of Wiley's first bookings on the parachute jumping circuit was in Maysville, where his family lived. W. J. Showen, editor of the *Maysville News*, promoted Wiley's visit. Up to that point Wiley had used made-up names while performing his jumps. Since he was coming home, he decided to use his real name for the first time. He showed up in Maysville on Monday and announced his jump for the next Sunday at a reduced rate of $75.

Maysville was abuzz over the flying circus of Wiley Post coming to town. Wiley stayed with his parents for the rest of the week and noticed that his father never talked about the jump scheduled for Sunday. William and Mae had no idea their son was working as a parachute jumper.

Wiley "took the family breath away" when he told them he was a jumper and was going to perform on Sunday. His father tried to dissuade him but his mother was so glad to see him that "it didn't

LEFT TO RIGHT – SADOWSKY, TIBBS, FRENCH
PARKER, POST, BEST, LEWIS

Wiley had barely learned to fly when he became a barnstormer for the "Texas Top-Notch Fliers," directed by veteran pilot Burrell Tibbs. Wiley, third from right, donned his flying goggles, to pose with Tibbs and other pilots of the flying circus. Billy Parker, later the director of aviation for Phillips Petroleum Company, is on Wiley's right. Courtesy Oklahoma Historical Society.

Wiley sits at the controls of Billy Parker's "Pusher," similar
to the bi-plane that Wiley learned to fly in while
barnstorming as a parachute jumper in 1926. Courtesy
Oklahoma Historical Society.

take much persuasion to induce her to get him to stop arguing"
with Wiley.[26]

Wiley hired Virgil Turnbull, a novice pilot from nearby Pauls
Valley, to take him up on Sunday. Wiley later recalled that Sunday
as the "worst setback" of his aviation career.

When he got home, he looked for his parachute to make certain "it was properly packed." It was gone! He looked in all the
closets, the attic, the outbuildings, and finally asked the neighbors.

He never saw that parachute again. His father was not too dis-
turbed about its disappearance and that made Wiley suspicious.
Wiley had to go to the men of the town "who were getting the
crowd out" and apologize. Wiley promised to get another parachute and be ready by the next week.[27]

Wiley promised the Maysville officials that nothing short of a tornado would stop him from jumping the next week. He traveled to Oklahoma City by train and borrowed a parachute. After a big Sunday dinner at his mother's house, the show began.

Wiley and his pilot circled over Maysville a couple of times and gave the folks "a little sideshow while the crowd was gathering"—a few loops and one slow roll. The rest was just climbing and diving. Wiley spent his time watching the gyrations of the dual-stick socket and the motions of the rudder pedals "as the plane dived, zoomed, and rolled about." He still had visions of getting enough money together to buy a plane and become a pilot.[28]

The jump went off "in good style" and even Mr. Post expressed his admiration of his son when he got home. Wiley Post was a hero in his hometown.

Wiley made a good living as a parachute jumper for almost two years. He made 99 jumps and thrilled crowds with dare-devil stunts like waiting until the last moment to open his chute and jumping with two parachutes.[29]

A mule stole the show from Wiley once during a Sunday afternoon barnstorming show at Hugo in southeastern Oklahoma. While free falling from 2,000 feet, Wiley spotted a mule in the meadow below. He frantically tried to avoid landing on the animal. However, when Wiley hit the ground, the parachute covered the head of the terrified mule that promptly turned and ran, dragging Wiley behind.

Wiley saw the bad side of humans during his parachute jumping days. He called his observations of people "studying crowd psychology." He realized that people were somehow thrilled when he delayed his parachute opening. He could feel their excitement that he was defying death.[30]

Wiley was shocked by the crowd's reaction after two of his friends died in a fiery crash of an old JN–4 during an airshow:

I shall never forget the smug satisfaction apparent in the crowd. At first I refused to believe it. Then, when I realized the truth, I spent the most miserable two weeks of my existence. To think that the spectators of airplane maneuvers were just a bloodthirsty mob that enjoyed watching men get killed was just a little more than I could stand. I got mad. I would show them.[31]

Wiley was so impressed by the whole affair that it revolutionized his technique in staging future flying exhibitions.

Wiley had about four hours of dual flying under his belt when he decided it was time to solo. Sam Bartel made Wiley put up $200 as security for the loan of his Canuck, a Curtiss JN–4 Jenny built in Canada, even though the plane was worth only about $150. Wiley's first solo was almost his last. "It wasn't until after I had wobbled down the rough ground and cleared the fence that I realized I was all alone in the plane," he recalled. For the first time in his life he was almost frightened.

He flew to an altitude where he felt comfortable and flew around for nearly half an hour before he felt "sufficiently sure of himself" to attempt a landing. Then he cut the gun, stuck the nose over and started down. He forgot to clear the motor out occasionally, and "the thing coughed and sputtered." Then he got really scared. Was his first solo to end in a forced landing?

He "shot the throttle forward." With some hesitation the engine caught again, but he neglected to pull the nose up soon enough. Almost immediately he was diving toward the ground so fast that "a third spasm of fright" paralyzed his mind. He discovered later that he had barely missed a tree with his right wing before he pulled the ship up again and circled for another landing.[32]

Wiley landed safely and took the plane up one more time before calling it a day. Bartel gave him back his deposit in full and accused Wiley of just showing off on the first landing attempt.

Wiley Post was now, officially. . . a real pilot.

Wiley worked as a parachute jumper and wingwalker with early pilot Tom Park in Ardmore. Park, later a successful commercial pilot with United Airlines, said he and Wiley parted company in a pasture in Ada when the big crowds simply stopped coming to the Sunday afternoon programs. The barnstorming business began running out of gas in 1925. Americans were accustomed to airplanes dotting the wild blue yonder. Planes were for sale everywhere. Wiley had his choice of many planes for $150, but he left them alone, believing the vintage planes to be "man-killers."

Everyone knew Wiley desperately wanted his own plane. Wherever he was working, he found a local airport to hang around in his spare time. He announced to anyone that would listen that he was destined to be a commercial pilot and he was going to buy himself a plane "any day now."

Pilot jobs were opening up all over. Private contractors hauled the mail and airline passenger service was offered to many of America's major cities. Wiley did not have enough experience to land one of the good jobs. He recognized that he needed to own his own airplane so he could build up enough hours to get a job in commercial aviation. He returned to the oilfields to earn enough money to buy his own plane, a move that almost cost him his career.

A MAJOR SETBACK

It was a bad time for my first forced landing—

WILEY POST

WILEY WENT TO WORK October 1, 1926, for $7 a day for Droppleman and Cuniff, an oil drilling company, on a rig near Seminole. He had worked for only a few hours toward his dream of saving money for his own airplane when a freak accident cost him his left eye.

A roughneck struck an iron bolt with a sledgehammer. A chip from the bolt lodged in Wiley's left eye. Dr. T. G. Wails tried to save the eye, but infection set in. A condition known as sympathetic ophthalmia resulted in the infection in the left eye causing loss of vision in Wiley's right eye. The decision was made to remove his left eye.[33]

Wiley was just short of his twenty-eighth birthday. With only one eye, how could he ever realize his dream to become a commercial pilot? He was an ex-convict with a sixth-grade education and no formal pilot training. When most men would have given up and changed careers, Wiley Post set his jaw more firmly than ever before toward his dream in aviation. Stanley Mohler and Dr. Bobby Johnson, in a 1971 Smithsonian Institution article on Post, attributed his motivation to three factors: inherent genius for aeronautics; a compelling urge to get into aviation; and steel-willed determination to accomplish an established objective.[34]

Wiley spent two months recuperating at his uncle's home in the Davis Mountains in southwest Texas. He was not discouraged and knew he could fly with one eye.

He had plenty of time to think. The sight of his right eye was gradually returning to normal and he practiced gauging depth on hills and trees. He would "look at a tree and try to guess its distance." Then he would step off the distance. He did the same with hills, and "timed his four-mile-an-hour gait" as a check on his judgment. At first, his mental calculations were far off, but by the end of the two months he was a better judge of distance than he had ever been.[35] Post was a champion in overcoming his handicap. And something good came of the accident—$1,800 for the loss of his eye, awarded by the Oklahoma State Industrial Court. After paying out expenses, Wiley had more than $1,200 left, a sufficient stake to purchase an airplane—at the expense of an eye!

Wiley began wearing a black patch over his eye, a symbol that became his trademark and made him easily recognizable all over the world in later years.

Great strides were made in American aviation in 1927. In the summer, Charles Augustus Lindbergh's solo flight across the Atlantic Ocean "struck a responsive chord in the minds of millions. . . and gave a tremendous boost to aviation."[36] "Lindy" was first to fly non-stop across the Atlantic. The world acclaimed him as a hero and he was commissioned a Colonel in the U. S. Air Service Reserve. He was a technical adviser to commercial airlines in the infancy of the American aviation industry.

Also in 1927, National Air Transport, Incorporated, initiated a passenger and freight service from Oklahoma City to Chicago, and Oklahoma City was on the country's first transcontinental air mail route which ran from Dallas-Fort Worth to Chicago. During this golden age of American aviation Wiley bought his first plane.

He paid $240 for a Canuck with a 90-horsepower OX-5 motor that had been slightly damaged in a crash. The Canuck was the Canadian version of the famous Curtiss JN–4 "Jenny" military training airplane of World War I. It became popular with barnstormers with its 60-mile-per-hour cruising speed and its ability to roll more rapidly than its American counterpart. The OX-5 engine was an eight-cylinder, water-cooled motor that used nine gallons of fuel per hour. The plane carried a 20-gallon fuel tank.

After shelling out $300 to Art Oakley at Ardmore for repairs, Wiley was ready for business when he painted the word "Post" below the rear cockpit. Through hard work, he built up a near monopoly in the flying business in his corner of the world. It was rough country in southeast Oklahoma, southern Arkansas, and northeast Texas. The lower end of the Ozarks flowed into the Kiamichi Mountains and flying was bad. "Lots of local fog, bad currents of air, and plenty of scrub timber" made emergency landings almost impossible. He hired out to flying circuses on Sundays and to oilmen who wanted to get to new leaseholdings quickly.[37]

Art Oakley had built a hangar and a crude landing field north of Ardmore after learning how to "mechanic" on airplanes during his service in the Army Air Corps in World War I. A master mechanic, he played a major role in the early years of Wiley's aviation career by keeping Wiley's plane flying and giving him occasional advanced flying lessons.

Oakley promoted Wiley by inviting him to barnstorm in Ardmore during "trade day," a local Chamber of Commerce promotion in which merchants were sold tiny advertising spaces on a leaflet announcing a barnstormer was coming to town. Both the merchants and the citizens of the town benefited when the leaflets were dropped from a low-flying airplane before an air show on Sunday afternoon.[38]

Wiley developed another interest in the spring of 1927 when he met 17-year-old Mae Laine while on a barnstorming tour in Sweetwater, Texas. Mae was 11 years younger than Wiley. Her father, rancher Dave Laine, had known the Posts when both families had lived years before in Grand Saline. Wiley described his meeting of Mae as his "first thrill aside from aviation." Mae was excited about flying and always showed up at air shows. Wiley's business began to suffer when he turned down weekend flying jobs so he could fly to Sweetwater to see Mae.

Wiley began to talk to Mae about marriage, but her parents strongly objected. They thought she was too young to marry and they did not cherish the thought of having an aviator for a son-in-law. Wiley and Mae decided to elope.

On June 27, 1927, "after the business of the day was over," the soon-to-be Mrs. Post and Wiley piled into the ship. Mae had a small bag with her and Wiley had a license in his pocket. Her father was not "favorably disposed" to the marriage so they decided to take the matter into their own hands. They fled the town.[39]

The escape from Sweetwater to Oklahoma was made in Wiley's $240 plane that had flown without incident for more than 800 hours since he bought it several months before. That is, until that important night.

Wiley and Mae were both "a little nervous," and his old companion, the plane, must have "got sympathetic tremors." Over Graham, Oklahoma, the rotor in the magneto distributor suddenly "ground itself to powder," and the gallant OX gasped and then quit.

It was a bad time for Wiley's first forced landing. He looked over at a cornfield where the "fodder was set in rows, cut and shocked." He headed for it and smacked down on the rough ground. "Bouncing along between two windrows, the wing tips overrode the tops of the shocks and lifted the plane a little," but fortunately the good old ship was strong enough to stand it.[40]

Wiley installed a rotor and found a local parson to marry the couple. There was no waiting period in Oklahoma and Wiley used the marriage license he had bought in Texas to make the union between Mae and him legal in the Sooner State. The first few hours of their honeymoon were spent removing the corn shocks from their "runway" in the corn field so the Canuck could once again take to the skies.

Wiley continued to barnstorm for two years after he and Mae were married. Mae became an integral part of the Post show. She carried his parachute on the bus as her luggage when Wiley wanted to make jumps at air shows. And it was Mae's responsibility to drive their car cross-country to provide ground transportation wherever Wiley was working. Mae said summers were great for barnstorming, but winters were lean. Since there were few, if any, airstrips for barnstormers, they often used fields and had to "walk the pastures" to check for rocks and gullies.

Wiley gave flying lessons on the side. Eula Pearl Carter Scott was only 12 when Wiley landed in her father's pasture at the north edge of Marlow and introduced her to the world of flying:

> He took my daddy up because he landed in his pasture and they knew each other real well. I was always a tomboy so I asked Wiley a hundred questions about this and that and then he took me up and when he did, he wanted to know if I wanted to hold the stick. I told him of course I did. So we flew for quite a while. That was my first lesson.[41]

Eula continued her lessons every time Wiley visited the Marlow area. She became so intrigued with flying that she convinced her father, George Carter, to buy her an airplane.

When a landing field and a hangar were completed, Mr. Carter asked Wiley to pick out an airplane. Eula knew what day Wiley was coming with her new plane. She was in school when she heard the airplanes coming over. Burrell Tibbs was flying Wiley's plane. She "could hardly sit still," but in a minute the principal came from the office and told her she was "wanted by daddy." She went to the office and there they were. Eula was thrilled to death.[42]

Once on a trip to Wyoming, Wiley learned firsthand about atmospheric pressure and the effects of temperature and altitude on the performance of his old Hispano-Standard airplane. He was hired to fly two ranchers about 200 miles to Cheyenne. It was high noon when Wiley took the plane and its heavy load of baggage up from a pasture 6,000 feet above sea level. He tried four times unsuccessfully to take off because the thin air would not support the plane.

Wiley needed the money he would make from the charter, so he unloaded much of the baggage and even some of his fuel. Still, he could only gain 100 feet of altitude before gliding back to the ground. Wiley could not complete his take off until late in the evening when the air cooled and increased in density. Wiley's on-the-job training in atmospheric conditions equipped him for major contributions to aviation later in his life.[43]

A major financial setback for Wiley came in 1927 when he seriously damaged his Canuck in a ground roll while on a hunting trip in Mexico. He brought the plane back to Ardmore where Art Oakley repaired it. However, Wiley did not have sufficient money to pay for the repairs and was forced to sell the plane to another flying enthusiast, J. Bart Scott, for $350. Wiley signed on with Scott as a flight instructor and barnstormer at Purcell, about 30 miles south of Oklahoma City.

Wiley and Mae moved into a small house in Purcell and suffered financially. Wiley earned a meager $3 per flight hour while instructing would-be pilots or giving airplane rides. There was no guarantee, so some days there was no pay.

Barnstorming jobs dried up by the winter of 1927 and Wiley went looking for a steady pilot's job. He heard about two Chickasha oil men, Florence C. Hall who went by "F. C." because he thought his parents had given him a girl's name, and Powell Briscoe, who were considering using an airplane in their business. Hall was conscious of timeliness in his business since he had once arrived later than a competitor and missed a lucrative oil deal.

Hall had scraped out a meager living in a drug store until he saved $250 to invest in an oil lease near Burkburnett, Texas, just after World War I. He worked the lease himself until he sold it for $35,000. After buying oil leases around Chickasha and teaming up with Briscoe, the Hall and Briscoe Company made $800,000 from the sale of a pipeline. Hall became a millionaire by successfully drilling oil wells in Grady and Carter counties in the 1920s.

Wiley camped out in Hall's office lobby for several days before the oil man agreed to see him. Wiley impressed Hall and Briscoe and was hired as their personal pilot for $200 a month. Wiley used part of his first paycheck to buy a new high-powered rifle to use on his frequent hunting trips.[44]

Hall and Briscoe bought a new 1928 three-place, open-cockpit Travel Air biplane manufactured in Wichita, Kansas. Wiley was well qualified to be the chief pilot, chauffeur and hunting companion for F. C. Hall. He knew Oklahoma's oil country like the back of his hand. He had flown so many barnstorming tours that he never needed a map if he flew in southern Oklahoma or north Texas. Wiley and Mae moved to an apartment in Oklahoma City, close to his new job in Chickasha.

Wiley was apprehensive about congressional passage of aeronautics legislation in 1926. Up to that time pilots were not required to obtain a government license. Wiley was fearful that, with one eye, he could not pass the physical examination required of commercial pilots. He often landed in small towns and out-of-the-way airports to avoid inspectors from the U.S. Department of Commerce Aeronautics Branch. The provision in the 1926 law that concerned Wiley was the requirement for "visual acuity of not less than 20/30 in each eye, although in certain instances less than 20/30 may be accepted if the applicant wears a correction to 20/30 in his goggles and has good judgment of distance without correction." The code also prohibited issuance of a pilot license to anyone with "organic disease of the eye, ear, nose or throat."[45]

Wiley found a loophole in the new law which allowed "waivers" to be granted to experienced aviators with physical defects. Wiley passed a test given to him by the Aeronautics Branch and flew 700 probationary hours before he was finally licensed with air transportation license number 3259, September 16, 1928.

Wiley became close to Hall and Briscoe. Briscoe later said that Wiley "didn't have a nerve in his body. When other people were scared, Wiley just grinned."[46] Hall became like a second father to Wiley. Hall was a very unusual man. Although he was a born gambler, he had, in Wiley's opinion, "about the best judgment of any man I have ever known." For many years he worked in a drug store in Texas. He was one of the first to "get into the swing of oil-leasing." Hall drilled more than 300 wells with only two dry holes. Wiley said Hall had a heart "as big as his bank account."[47]

Wiley safely flew Hall and Briscoe all over the oil fields of Oklahoma and Texas. Once they encountered a vicious rainstorm near Shamrock in the Texas panhandle. Wiley landed with his nervous passengers in a rough pasture. No one was injured but one of the plane's struts was broken. Wiley patched up the plane with wire and a two-by-four and the trip continued.

THE WINNIE MAE

She was about the last word in airplanes—

W I L E Y   P O S T

F. C. HALL had two hobbies—aviation and his daughter, Winnie Mae, who traveled with her father and Wiley all across the mid-section of America. By 1928 the Halls grew weary of their three-seat, open-cockpit Travel Air. Cabin planes were improving every day, and the Hall family soon decided they were tired of getting "all dressed up like magazine aviators just to travel a few hundred miles." Late in 1928, Hall sent Wiley to the Lockheed factory in Los Angeles to turn in the Travel Air for a new Lockheed Vega. Wiley was overjoyed because the new ship was to be one of those airplanes that could "go places and see things."[48]

Hall had been introduced to the Vega by Allan Loughhead (the original spelling of Lockheed) and Norman Hall of Lockheed who made a 2,500 mile journey through Texas and Oklahoma, trying to sell their new plane to oil men.

The Vega was named Winnie Mae after Hall's daughter. It was a new kind of airplane for America. It had a smooth and tough plywood fuselage that provided an aerodynamically clean surface for faster flying; its wings and tailgroup were braced from inside, eliminating the wires and struts that were needed in earlier planes; it was designed to carry heavier loads; it was equipped with a Wasp air-cooled radial engine; and it was more difficult to stall in flight.

Wiley traveled to the Lockheed plant in Burbank, California, to pick up the Winnie Mae, the most up-to-date airplane of 1928.

Wiley's 1930 pilot's license issued by the Federation Aeronautique Internationale. The license was signed by Orville Wright. Courtesy Oklahoma Historical Society.

Wiley was like a kid with a new toy, "After Canucks, Jennies, and the Travel Air, sitting at the stick behind that Wasp was like changing from a slow freight to a limited express. It was so sensitive and responsive to the controls that it seemed to anticipate my moves. And as for comfort—well, once one gets used to riding indoors, an open ship is just an old crate, no matter how good it may be otherwise."[49]

Wiley made several test flights with the Winnie Mae before returning to Oklahoma City. Mr. Hall and Winnie Mae were just as happy and proud as Wiley when he roared over the airport fence at Oklahoma City with the new ship. Wiley "pulled up in a steep climb" to show off the tricks of the white bullet and then put her through her paces high in the air so that her new owner might see what a beautiful thing his Winnie Mae was.[50]

The name "Mae" played a major role in Wiley's life. His mother, his wife, and his airplane were all named Mae. A friend once said that if Wiley had a daughter, surely her name would have been Mae.

Everything was going great for Hall's oil investments until the Great Depression hit Oklahoma and the nation right between the eyes. It began with the stock market crash of 1929 and worsened as banks failed, stores and factories closed their doors, and millions of Americans were left homeless and jobless.

Oklahoma suffered severely. The state economy was based largely on agriculture, and the plight of the farmer was a weakness of the American economy during the 1920s, a weakness which contributed both to the severity and the length of the Depression.

The weather contributed to Oklahoma's economic problems. A searing drought hit even the normally wet eastern third of the state. Oklahoma was wracked with dust storms. Sand blew in such storms that travelers lost their way, chickens went to roost at noon, airports closed, and trains stopped. Animals and humans alike suffered lung disorders.

All 77 counties in Oklahoma were designated disaster areas and were eligible for federal drought assistance. Oklahoma farmers quit the land and moved to town to hunt for jobs that many times were not available. Farm foreclosures were daily events. Only two states had a higher percentage of agricultural workers on public assistance rolls. Oklahoma's population decreased by almost one-million over the next 20 years.[51]

Hall and Briscoe could not afford to keep Wiley on the payroll and pay the substantial costs associated with owning a fine airplane. The oil men had decided to sell the Vega back to Lockheed, but Wiley had another idea. Colonel William Easterwood of Dallas had offered a $50,000 prize for anyone who could fly the Pacific Ocean from Dallas to Hong Kong with only one fuel stop. Believing he could make it with the *Winnie Mae*, Wiley began to work out details for the crossing. However, Colonel Easterwood withdrew his offer and the *Winnie Mae* was sold to Lockheed. The name was painted out and the aircraft was sold to Nevada Airlines.

Wiley flew the farewell flight of the airplane to California and landed an unexpected job as a test pilot for Lockheed. He was given a good salary and flew a demonstration and sales tour in Washington and Oregon in early 1929.

Wiley worked at Lockheed less than a year, but it was time well spent. He daily rubbed shoulders with some of the world's best aeronautical engineers, whose names are familiar with enthusiasts of aviation: Jack Northrop, Gerald Vultee, Allan Lockheed, and Richard Palmer. Lockheed was a small company, with only 50 employees, and Wiley gained much technical knowledge of aircraft design and flight-test procedures.

The *Winnie Mae* was not completely out of Wiley's life. Since he worked at Lockheed, which now owned the plane, he flew his old ship as escort for women pilots in the 1929 National Air Races competition in the Santa Monica-Cleveland Derby. It was there he met for the first time another pilot, a woman, Amelia Earhart.

Earhart was born the same year as Wiley, 1898. She grew up in Kansas but was well educated at Columbia University and Harvard University. In 1928 she was the first woman to make a transatlantic crossing as a passenger. In 1932 she became the first woman to fly across the Atlantic, and in 1935, the first woman to fly the Pacific Ocean, crossing from Hawaii to California. In a flight around the world in 1937, Earhart and navigator Fred Noonan disappeared while en route from New Guinea to Howland Island. Their fate remains a mystery six decades later.

In the 1929 race, Earhart flew a Lockheed Vega and finished third. Louis Thaden was first in a Travel Air. In her book *Last Flight,* Earhart gave credit to Wiley for helping her plan strategy for her long-distance flights in 1934 and 1935.

Wiley added hundreds of hours to his logbook during his employment at Lockheed. He ferried airplanes from California eastward and from Texas to Mexico. He even obtained a pilot's license from the Mexican government in 1929. He competed for the 1929 Edsel B. Ford Reliability Trophy, part of the National Air Tour. Even though his plane averaged the fastest speeds in the race, the formula for points penalized the Vega so winning was impossible before he began. But Wiley said he "had a lot of fun taking off last on 200-mile runs and getting in in first place."[52]

One incident in California demonstrated just how accurately Wiley had trained his good eye. One day he argued in a friendly manner with James Harold "Jimmy" Doolittle, Carl Squier, General Manager of Lockheed, Roscoe Turner, and Marshall Headle, Lockheed's chief test pilot, about who had the best vision. When they looked out the window in Squier's office, Wiley could read signs at such long distances that no one else could make them out. The group did not believe Wiley until they walked down the street, nearer the signs. Wiley had read each sign accurately.

Doolittle would cross paths with Wiley many times in the next few years. Doolittle was a gunnery and flight instructor in World War I and served as chief of experimental flying for the U.S. Army Air Corps after the war. In 1922 he became the first pilot to fly across the United States in less than a day. He rose to the rank of Lieutenant General in the U. S. Air Force and is best known for leading the first U. S. air raid on Japan during World War II. Doolittle died in 1993.

In June, 1930, Wiley received a call from his old employer, F. C. Hall. Times were better for Hall and he wanted another airplane. The original *Winnie Mae* had been sold so Hall asked Wiley to order a new Vega and add any improvements he had designed. Hall said, "I want a new ship, and I'll let you make some of those flights you were figuring on last year."

Wiley was excited about working for Hall again and jubilant about his new airplane, a $22,000 seven-passenger monoplane with a 420-horsepower Pratt and Whitney Wasp engine.

It was a great day when the new plane came off the line. She was "about the last word in airplanes," according to Wiley who took her up to test and recommended a few changes. As soon as the changes were made Wiley "tore out of Los Angeles" with Mae beside him and "made the air hot with the skin friction of the wings, making tracks back to Oklahoma City."[53]

The new *Winnie Mae* was a class airplane. It had a 150-gallon fuel tank, an electric inertia starter, and was painted white, with purple trim. The plane was 27 feet long and had a wingspan of 41 feet. It could cruise comfortably from 150 to 190 miles per hour.

Wiley was glad to be based back in Oklahoma but his old desire to make a record flight "took a tight hold" on him. Hall approved of Wiley's plan to make a transcontinental flight. Soon the men who ran the National Air Races in Chicago announced a non-stop derby between Los Angeles and Chicago. Wiley knew his plane was fast enough to win so he went about making more changes in the ship.

He had the wing set at a little lower angle of incidence to lessen the resistant forces at high speeds. Knowing that he would have to land it "with the tail well down, giving the wing a high angle of attack at slow speeds," he had four inches taken off the tail skid. This was to prevent the tail bouncing on landings and tossing the ship over on its nose. He had tanks installed to bring the fuel capacity up to more than 500 gallons, and by the time he was through testing and adjusting the ship and engine, more than 10 miles an hour had been added to her originally fast top speed.[54]

Wiley asked Harold Gatty, an Australian navigator living in California, to lay out the 1,760-mile course from Los Angeles to Chicago. Gatty's incredible ability as a navigator was later described by Will Rogers:

> He can take a $1.00 Ingersoll watch, a Woolworth compass, and a lantern, and at twelve o'clock at night he can tell you just how many miles the American farmer is away from the poor house. He can look at the North Star and a Southern Democrat and tell you if Oklahoma will go Republican, or sane. He knows the moon like a lobbyist knows Senators. Give him one peek at the Giant Dipper, the 86th Meridian, and the Northampton, Massachusetts, mail carrier's bag, and he can tell you if Calvin [Coolidge] will run again.[55]

Wiley thought he could win the race to Chicago, refuel and complete a transcontinental flight on to New York. Gatty worked all night before the start of the race and pushed his maps and charts into Wiley's hands just before takeoff. It was Wiley's first experience flying with accurate navigational data, he had always flown by the seat of his pants. He gave Gatty the credit for winning the race, "Gatty's charts led me straight over the course, and my tail was being pushed by a good wind. All of a sudden I saw my compass start swinging. Then it stuck. I had no other with me, so I had to navigate from the map. The misfortune made me lose about 40 minutes on the flight. Even then, I still beat my nearest rival of the day into the field by 11 seconds."[56]

The *Winnie Mae* averaged 192 miles an hour, a new record of nine hours, nine minutes, and four seconds.[57]

Wiley abandoned his plans to fly on to New York. Because of the 40-minute loss due to the broken compass, it would have been almost impossible to get to New York in time to beat the 12-hour, 25-minute record of Captain Frank Hawk. Wiley was satisfied with the $7,500 prize for winning the derby.

The next day, Wiley got a thrill, "A plane like mine grew out of the west, took shape, and flashed across the finish line. The judges computed its time and declared it had beaten the plane which had followed me in to second place the day before. The new bidder for derby honors was Art Goebel, former holder of the transcontinental record. And what ship do you think he was flying? You bet! The old *Winnie Mae*."[58]

Repainted a bit, slightly changed, and under a new boss, the old *Winnie Mae* was still the good old airplane in which Wiley had spent so many hours.[59]

Wiley compared notes with Goebel and discovered that both had used Harold Gatty for navigational help. It was an incredible fact that the fastest two commercial airplanes in America in 1930 were both *Winnie Mae*'s.

Wiley predicted to his friends that Gatty would help him achieve his life-long dream. . . to fly around the world:

> That clinched the slight little Australian with me. He was going around the world with me, although he didn't know it at that time. I would take him if I had to shanghai him![60]

Part
Two

A NEW CHALLENGE

I tried to keep my mind a total blank—

W I L E Y   P O S T

BY THE AUTUMN of 1930, cross-country flying had become monotonous to Wiley. The steady grind of ferrying his employer, F. C. Hall, from one bad landing field surrounded by oil derricks to another, was beginning to wear on Wiley's spirit of adventure. He wanted to fly around the world:

> I don't remember ever hearing much about Magellan when I was a kid, and even the Cabots are pretty dim recollections, but I still get a kick out of my old history book which shows a picture of Columbus looking out to sea. Columbus thought he was going around the world to Asia, and just that phrase "going around the world" had a great thrill for me, especially as my view of the world was the flat horizon of Texas.[61]

From the beginning of his employment with Hall, it was understood that Wiley needed latitude to make special flights in the interest of aviation. The Depression had slowed Hall's business and Wiley was not needed full-time as a pilot. The time was right for Wiley Post to fly around the world.

Aviation needed something original to stimulate passenger business. The impetus, begun in 1927, had resulted in the nation's being covered by elaborate networks of airlines. But there was still the "bugaboo of the flying hazard," and the public needed more definite proof of the reliability of the airplane under all conditions.[62]

Wiley's "something original" had to be an around-the-world flight in record time. Transcontinental flying in the United States had been conquered by Frank Hawk. The coasts were now just over 12 hours apart. Charles Lindbergh had flown across the Atlantic. Only "circling the globe" would fulfill Wiley's dream.

By 1931 three around-the-world flights had been successfully completed. In 1924 the U. S. Army's World Fliers, in two open-cockpit biplanes, Douglas DWC World Cruisers, circled the globe over a six month span from April 6 to September 28. Their trip began and ended in Seattle. In August, 1929, the German airship Graf Zeppelin circumnavigated the earth in just 21 days. Wiley

Wiley (left) and Harold Gatty spent months in the spring and summer of 1931 preparing for their journey around the earth in the Winnie Mae. Gatty meticulously mapped out the trip while Wiley made certain the airplane was mechanically in tip-top shape. Courtesy Oklahoma Historical Society.

was impressed, "It had done what Columbus might have accomplished, had he not bumped into the North American continent on the way. It had reduced the time taken by Magellan, the first globe-circler, by more than three years."[63]

Even though the Zeppelin had a long record of service, and was overshadowing the airplane in the public's mind from the standpoint of safety, Wiley predicted the demise of the dirigible, "Looking at the log of the huge, and to my mind, lumbering airship, I was convinced that that type of transportation would never supersede other forms of air transport. Speed has been the keynote of air transportation developments since the beginning of the wheel-and-axle days. Safety has been more or less secondary to speed."[64]

What Wiley was ready and anxious to prove was that "a good airplane with average equipment and careful flying" could outdo the Graf Zeppelin or any other similar aircraft, at every turn on a flight around the world.

Wiley hoped to cut in half the time the Zeppelin had taken. His goal was to fly from New York to New York, east to west, in ten days.

His equipment consisted of one airplane, "the fastest load-carrier" he had ever seen, and the promised backing of Mr. Hall, in addition to the few thousand dollars he had saved. Wiley had seven years' training in flying, "mostly of the hardest sort." He knew from past experience a navigator who could chart a course for him. That navigator was Harold Gatty.[65]

Hall agreed to allow Wiley to use the *Winnie Mae* on the trip, with certain conditions. Wiley could not accept commercial endorsements of equipment or merchandise. Wiley wondered how he could make the trip break even without some kind of endorsement, but he left the business side of the venture to Hall.

In mid-January, 1931, Wiley flew the *Winnie Mae* to Los Angeles to enlist the help of Harold Gatty, whom he thought was a necessity for a successful flight. Gatty said yes, looking upon the projected flight as an excellent opportunity to try out several of his innovative theories of aerial navigation.

Gatty was three years younger than Wiley and had a wealth of experience as a navigator. He had been trained at the Royal Australian Naval College and assisted dozens of fliers all over the world in long-distance flights. He ran a navigation school in California and had taught many fliers, including Art Goebel and Anne Morrow Lindbergh. In 1930 he was part of Harold Bromley's unsuccessful attempt to fly the Pacific. Storms and fog turned them back to Japan after covering much of their route. Gatty had collected massive amounts of meteorological and geographical information. He was extremely knowledgeable of airfields and flying conditions in the Orient, Siberia, and Alaska. Wiley was glad to have Gatty on his team. In fact, he was so impressed with Gatty's vast storehouse of knowledge he felt free to leave that side of the preparation to Gatty and devote all his time to the practical engineering and mechanical end of the flight.[66]

Wiley left Gatty and his books and flew back to Oklahoma City to begin training his body and his mind for the "long grind ahead." He did not want to cause delays on the trip because of mental fatigue or physical incapacity.

As Wiley flew about the country in the regular routine of his job he tried his best to keep his mind "a total blank." That may sound easy, but it was one of the hardest things Wiley ever had to do. According to his theory, it was of primary importance in overcoming one of the greatest dangers on the flight, "slowed-up reactions at the end of a long hop," that might easily result in ground-looping or some other form of minor accident in landing. By keeping his mind a blank, he piloted the aircraft automatically, without mental effort, "letting my actions be wholly controlled by my subconscious."[67]

Wiley began preparing his body for the demanding trip around the world. He knew he had to control his sleeping habits so he changed his hours of sleep every day for months before the trip, in hopes of developing the ability to sleep at available times to avoid acute fatigue, the enemy of all long-distance pilots. He found by limiting his intake of food, he did not need as much sleep.

Wiley employed Lockheed to make some modifications on the

Winnie Mae. The starter was removed to save weight; the engine, having logged 245 hours, was overhauled; the tail skid was shortened by four inches to lessen the tendency for the fast-landing plane to nose-over; a special hatch in the top of the fuselage, with a folding windshield, was added so Gatty could use the stars for navigation; and the tanks were revamped.

While Wiley worked on getting the airplane mechanically perfect, Gatty gathered weather data from even the remotest points along the flight plan and invented a special combination wind-drift and ground-speed indicator to assist in navigation.

Ground speed was calculated by comparing the rate of passage of terrain, as viewed through an eyepiece and two prisms, with the rate of passage of a series of red marks placed on a film strip, moved by a clock mechanism at a fixed speed. The eyepiece was raised or lowered until the two rates were optically the same. Gatty then read off the distance above the film to which the eyepiece had been moved and consulted a table he had previously made in test flights with the airplane at known altitudes and ground speeds. The instrument was useful over land or water. The instrument was mounted near Gatty's seat in the *Winnie Mae.*[68]

Wiley and Mae closed their apartment in Chickasha and headed west to the Lockheed factory in Los Angeles in January, 1931, Wiley's first step toward his greatest adventure. It would take months of painstaking preparations to assure a safe and successful flight.

First, there was the matter of proper load alignment on the *Winnie Mae.* Wiley had Gatty make up a list of all he would need in the way of luggage, instruments, and other supplies on the trip, information needed to lay out the plan of loading the plane and placing fuel tanks to balance the ship so it could be properly trimmed for "flying at its maximum speed."[69]

The weight problem was a complex one because Wiley needed tanks that would hold 500 gallons of fuel, enough to make the longest hop on the trip of 2,550 miles. Wiley knew that it was up to him, as the pilot, to get the last ounce of efficiency from his airplane. Every extra five pounds on the airplane would cut air speed.

To make room for extra fuel tanks, Wiley modified the cockpit, "The interior of the cockpit was all fixed up to my taste, and it is a good thing that comfort was the word. I replaced the customary straight-backed steel "bucket" with a nice room armchair. It was a trifle short for leg room perhaps, but quite restful."[70]

Wiley had plenty of room to shift positions without getting too far from the controls. He needed room to keep from getting stiff during the 20 or more hours he might fly in one leg. Cordoned off from the cabin by the tanks which extended to the sides and top of the fuselage, Wiley had to enter and leave through the trapdoor on the roof. He was completely cut off from the rear.

Wiley took advice from some of the great aviation experts of the day on what instruments he needed on the *Winnie Mae*. Jimmy Doolittle, the famous aerobatic and fighter pilot who had pioneered the "blind flight takeoff and landing" radio and instrument system in 1929, suggested grouping three flying instruments, the rate-of-climb meter, the artificial gyroscopic horizon, and the bank-and-turn indicator, so that Wiley's eyes and other senses would be coordinated best. Roger Q. Williams, who had flown the Atlantic with Lewis Yancy in 1929, also advised Wiley on the best instruments available at the time. Wiley knew instruments would make or break his record attempt around the world.[71]

Gatty worked long hours in preparing for the trip. For each leg of the flight he made up charts and plotted courses from every bit of data he could collect in four short months of preparation.[72]

Gatty's seat was left unattached so that it could be moved forward or backward, depending on what load shifting was necessary as fuel was burned off during the flight. Gatty built a special speaking tube so he and Wiley could communicate. If the engine noise drowned out voices in the cabin, notes could be pulled through the tube by a wire.

With all the technical details taken care of, Wiley and Gatty turned to the political problems of making a trip around the world. In 1931 the United States had yet to officially recognize the Russian government, precluding any American fliers from touching down on Russian soil (The U.S. would not officially recognize

Russia until 1933).Wiley called on a fellow Oklahoman, Secretary of War Patrick Hurley (the only Oklahoman to serve as a member of the President's cabinet). Hurley knew diplomatic Washington well and worked with U.S. Senator William Borah of Idaho in getting at least unofficial permission from Russian officials for the *Winnie Mae* to land in their vast country.

Wiley and Gatty also visited the embassies of Japan, Poland, China, the Netherlands, Germany, and Great Britain, to obtain permission to fly over or land in their countries.

F. C. Hall was overly optimistic about how much money could be made from the around-the-world flight. He predicted that Post would make $75,000 from the flight alone and another $100,000 from barnstorming tours. Hall also thought that advertising from the "test" parts carried on the plane would bring in another $125,000. Gatty was guaranteed $5,000 and 25% of the take. Both pilot and navigator planned to take along stacks of autographed envelopes they hoped to have postmarked in each country and sell when they returned to America.

Hall hired the public relations firm of Dick Blythe and Harry Bruno to assist the fliers with the media. Blythe and Bruno, both early pilots, had assisted Charles Lindbergh in his 1927 flight. Exclusive rights to day-by-day coverage of the flight were sold to the *New York Times,* which promised its readers "a real scoop" in aviation history.[73] Hall also signed an agreement with Pathe News, a newsreel service, that provided Gatty with a motion picture camera and boxes of film.

All preparations were complete. Hall and his daughter, Winnie Mae, and her husband, Leslie Fain, traveled by train to New York to be present for the takeoff. Mae Post stayed in Oklahoma City with family members and planned to join her husband in New York upon completion of the trip.

On May 23, Wiley and Gatty landed at Roosevelt Field in New York. Now all they needed was good weather.

READY TO GO

The weather must improve sooner or later—

D R .   J A M E S   K I M B A L L

ROOSEVELT FIELD was named for President Theodore Roosevelt's son, Quentin, who was killed as a pilot in World War I. The field had been the site of much of America's civil aviation history by 1931. It was there that Charles Lindbergh launched his trans-Atlantic flight in 1927 and Rene Fonck crashed on takeoff in his attempt of a non-stop flight from New York to Paris a year later.

What lay ahead for Wiley and Gatty was a 15,000 mile flight plan that ran across the North Atlantic, to Berlin and Moscow, across the vast expanse of Siberia with its unpredictable weather patterns, across the Bering Straight to Alaska, then across Canada and back to New York. Associated Press writer Oscar Leiding compared the flight to the fictional adventure of Jules Verne, "Jules Verne sent mythical Phileas Fogg around the world in 80 days. Two hardy fliers hope to make the trip in one tenth, or maybe one-eighth of the time."[74]

Wiley and Gatty publicly announced they would be happy with a new world record of ten days, but they secretly hoped to complete the trip in eight, maybe even seven days.

Hours turned into days, and days into weeks, as Wiley and Gatty waited for favorable weather conditions to cross the Atlantic. Gatty later reflected on the waiting, "None of the trials we had during our months of preparation was as great as the long days and nights of waiting to take off from Roosevelt Field. When we landed there, our enthusiasm was at its highest peak. Daily we approached the final test of our plan. but as the weeks wore on, the continued bad-weather reports from distant and watery spots on the relentless North Atlantic wore us thin with impatience, and we soon developed that nervous tension which comes from enforced idleness and delayed anticipations."[75]

Wiley stayed busy adding new dials on his instrument board. Gatty, with dustcloth in hand, stayed near the *Winnie Mae*. "We felt the plane might develop lazy habits if we let her idle much longer. Dust collected on her nice white skin, and I began to check and recheck the instruments just to have something to do with my time."[76]

Several times it looked as if the weather would break so Wiley and Gatty loaded up their gear and sat on the runway, ready to go. Time after time, the weather report slammed the door shut on takeoff that day.

Wiley met daily with Dr. James K. Kimball, a U. S. Weather Bureau meteorologist in New York City. Kimball had become known as the "guardian angel" of aviators with his relentless forecasting of weather a thousand miles from Roosevelt Field over the Atlantic. Kimball was accustomed to fliers wanting his approval to take off even in less-than-favorable conditions.

Bad weather continued to plague the North Atlantic. A week before the Post-Gatty flight finally was launched, Wiley and Gatty tried to convince Kimball to give them the go-ahead, that Wiley's proficiency as a pilot and his ability to fly blind through fog and clouds would make a difference. Kimball patiently replied, "In my experience I have noticed a sharp division between the judicious application of courage and the foolhardiness of overconfidence. So why not be sensible about it? The weather must improve sooner or later."[77]

Wiley and Gatty took Kimball's advice, at least for the moment, but the nightly trek back to the Biltmore Hotel became more toilsome each day. Gatty described Wiley's condition in Dr. Kimball's office on top of Manhattan's 17 Battery Place:

From the meteorologist's office on top of the Whitehall Building overlooking the Battery and Upper New York Bay, Wiley's good eye looked out with alternate longing and anger. Stoical in the face of bad weather, the Statue of Liberty remained adamant to his pleadings for her to turn to the northeast and cast her beam over the Great Circle Course.[78]

The foggy weather lingered. Gatty decided he would be the cautious member of the team and be a restraining influence on Wiley's enthusiastic optimism.

With sobriety dampening their enthusiasm somewhat, they held another conference the next morning in Dr. Kimball's office. The day was clear and cool, and they agreed not to "try a start" until he gave the word that the fog area was less than an hour's run in thickness.[79]

After midnight on June 20, their spirits rose as good weather looked like a possibility. Wiley and Gatty packed their bags, left the Biltmore, and snatched some shuteye between weather reports from Kimball's office. The *Winnie Mae* was fully gassed up. Colonel Lindbergh called and wished them Godspeed. It looked like a "go." Only one potential storm racing east from Hudson Bay could spoil the takeoff. Gatty felt they had to beat that storm through. They could not afford to take any chances of delay at Harbor Grace, Newfoundland. However, the storm beat the adventurers to the takeoff, and "nobody benefited except the phone company." Plunged in gloom, they went back to bed with bitter thoughts.[80]

The next night they tried again, with no luck. Both men lost sleep to constant phone calls to the weather bureau and interviews with the dozens of reporters on hand to cover the event.

The endless posing for photographers was tiring. The "eerie light effects from the calcium flares" were almost blinding, and the acrid smoke from them hung low in the damp air and rain. It was stifling. The airport lights "danced in the prisms they made" through the sheets of rain which increased every minute.[81]

It seemed as if most of the world's pilots wanted to set some sort of record in 1931. On June 22, a woman pilot, Ruth Nichols, left Roosevelt field to attempt a non-stop flight to Paris. However, she overran the runway at her first stop at Harbor Grace, Newfoundland, and crashed. The *New York Times* reported that "An apparent injury to her spine, caused when she was tossed against the sharp corners of the fuel tanks in the cabin, became grave and had a serious effect on her nervous system." The plane was reduced to "20 percent of its former perfection" and was what is known to fliers as a "washout."

Early on the morning of June 23, a month after Wiley and Gatty landed at Roosevelt Field, weather conditions over the Atlantic finally permitted the beginning of the much-awaited flight. Gatty was anxious and excited. Wiley was not.

Calm old Wiley! He plunged through the rain in a borrowed raincoat. One would have thought he was going to take Mr. Hall off on a 100-mile hop and had lots of time. The zero hour came. Then Wiley used his head. With that rain it would have been impossible to be sure on the takeoff. Looking through the diamond-like drops on the windshield at the brilliant lights of the airport would distort everything. He refused to risk our months of effort on a few drops of rain and a few seconds of rushing along the ground at 70 miles an hour.[82]

Wiley decided to wait until dawn, two hours away. They left the plane and took shelter in an old shed, joined by friends and photographers and at least four other aviators waiting to fly across the Atlantic. It seemed as if the rain would never stop. As the first beams of daylight came, the rain came down worse than ever. The roof of the shed echoed the pounding rain. After posing for newsmen one more time, Wiley and Gatty climbed into the *Winnie Mae*. Gatty heard Wiley's cheery and sharp "Gas on; switch off." The reply from the mechanic, "Contact!", was so sharp that it rang in Gatty's ears even after the engine's low roar began.[83]

A *New York Times* reporter observed:

> For a few moments the big motor warmed up, a blue flame
> tongue from the exhaust occasionally licking out from under
> the cowling. Then its roar grew deeper. Slowly the plane crept
> ahead a foot or two and the pilot gave it a little more 'gun,'
> then began to taxi. Last-minute flares and flashes from
> photographers threw the whole scene into brilliance as the fliers
> waved goodbye through cockpit and cabin windows.[84]

One of the newspaper photographers, Herbert McCrory of the
New York Daily News, received burns to his hand and arm when
his flashlight powder exploded prematurely.

The plane taxied to the northeast corner of Roosevelt Field
over the bumpy, slippery grass. Gatty would never forget the takeoff, "I sucked in my breath as Wiley gave the Wasp all the throttle
it could take. Friends, field, and fences swept by the tiny windows
as we flashed along the runway. One bounce, a second lighter one,
and the plane hit the last with a heave and bounded into the
air."[85]

Gatty turned to his table and made the first entry into his log,
"Tuesday, June 23, 8:55:21. Took off 4:55 daylight-saving time,
set course 63 degrees, visibility poor."

Wiley glanced at his watch as he guided the *Winnie Mae* into
the still-dark sky, the sun still hidden beyond the eastern horizon
over the Atlantic. Wiley Post's big chance of breaking a world aviation record was underway, at last!

Back home in Maysville, Wiley's parents looked to the sky and
wondered how their son was faring. The Associated Press sent a reporter to the Post farm home and dispatched a story:

> In a little southern Oklahoma farm home, the elderly parents of
> Wiley Post tonight awaited news of their son's progress across
> the Atlantic in his aerial globe-girdling adventure with Harold
> Gatty. There is no telephone in the Post home and any message
> must be borne by courier.[86]

ON TO HARBOR GRACE

I worked fast and Wiley kept on climbing—

H A R O L D   G A T T Y

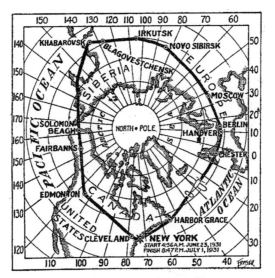

Route of Wiley and Gatty's around-the-world trip, 1931,
courtesy *The Daily Oklahoman*.

Wiley held the *Winnie Mae* at 400 feet to keep the ground in sight as he and Gatty left New York, headed for Harbor Grace, Newfoundland. The rain running down the windshield made it difficult to see. Wiley settled back to the business of trying to break the around-the-world record held by the Graf Zeppelin.

The arms on the big chair Wiley had put in the cockpit seemed to "yawn" with him as he tipped back. He began to wish that he "could get some altitude" that would let him forget the stick and fly the ship on the stabilizer and rudder. At 400 feet, things happened too fast for "one to let go of the stick."[87]

On the *Winnie Mae* flew, across the marshes and hills of Connecticut. The old Wasp engine performed perfectly and sang a sweet song in Wiley's ears. Soon they left the coast of Maine and headed for Nova Scotia. The world below was acutely aware of the fliers' attempt at the record. Two men in a fishing boat waved at the plane as she droned on.

Wiley had inestimable faith in the *Winnie Mae*. Gatty got a sample of Wiley's ability to handle her in her tricky moods when the rough air bounced the craft around off the Maine coast. Gatty spent a lot of his time grabbing the delicate instruments that crowded his table in the back of the plane.

Wiley was anxious to get the first leg of the trip under his belt so he jumped the *Winnie Mae's* speed up to 180 knots. Six hours and 47 minutes after taking off from Roosevelt Field, he caught sight of the airfield at Harbor Grace. Newfoundlanders had cleared the runway of stumps and boulders just four years before, after the site was selected as a link between America and Europe for daring aviators. Ruth Nichols, who had crashed the day before, was one of the aviators who had contributed money for the construction of the airport. The *New York Times* described the airfield:

> Back of rock-ribbed barren bluffs that face the blue bay and
> under which the town nestles, they have constructed a 4,000
> foot runway between the hills. They picked a mountain pasture
> covered with rocks and blueberry bushes and with immense
> labor moved stones enough to build a skyscraper and rooted
> out the bushes.[88]

Wiley circled once and headed for the runway that was located back from the fiord. He turned the nose of the plane toward the field and yanked back the throttle. He told Gatty, "Get as far back toward the tail as you can, kid." Gatty shifted his weight toward the tail and the nose drifted up, level. They lost altitude slowly and touched down softly to a tiny group of photographers and local onlookers.

Wiley and Gatty jumped out quickly and "made for food." Some photographers wanted to take their time with a lot of posing but were asked to wait until after lunch. Wiley felt the photographers deserved the pictures, "They had come all the way from New York, taking 5½ days by ordinary means of travel to get there, while we had made it in six hours and 47 minutes."[89]

Newfoundlanders did not get overly excited about trans-Atlantic flights that were almost a weekly occurrence in 1931. A few farm boys galloped their stocky ponies, "hardly bigger than the great Newfoundland dogs," across the moors to the airport and possibly a hundred citizens from the town fringing the bay itself would drive or "trudge up the twisting white roads" to the head of the runway. The fact that daring fliers were taking their lives in their hands over the North Atlantic did not particularly excite these folk, who have been accustomed throughout their history to "violent and sudden destruction at the whim of the North Atlantic."[90]

Herman Archibald, "a tall white-haired man with youthful, energetic steps," strode out with a megaphone in hand to meet the fliers and then took them to his sister's house for a hot meal.

Wiley and Gatty's first stop on their 1931 trip around the earth was at Harbor Grace, Newfoundland. Many of the island's inhabitants gathered at the primitive landing field to watch the *Winnie Mae* land on its first leg of an incredible adventure. Courtesy Oklahoma Historical Society.

While Wiley and Gatty were eating, Archibald recited the history of Harbor Grace. In his quick, clipped Newfoundland speech he said that the people believed with utmost faith that aviation was to be the salvation of a dying community. Not so many years ago Conception Bay was continually filled with a hundred or more ships. But now the blue bay was "dotted only by a scant sail or two, and the people are in hard straits."[91]

Wiley was in a hurry and asked Archibald to drive Gatty and him back to the airport. The local police had roped off the area around the *Winnie Mae* that was being refueled under the supervision of Ted Carlyle, a mechanic from Pratt and Whitney, the manufacturer of the Wasp engine. Gatty used the tail of the airplane for a table and began calculating the next leg of the trip. Wiley completed his pre-flight inspection, as described by Gatty:

> With maddening thoroughness he moved about, but the precision of his movements inspired confidence in me as I watched. Not a motion was wasted and not a square inch of the vital parts of the plane escaped his inspection. With borrowed pliers he tightened fuel couplings, tested vents, and got oil all over himself, so that he looked like a "grease-monkey" when he finally stood on the spat of the wheel for a last pose in front of the suppliant photographers.[92]

Wiley spent ten full minutes warming up and testing the engine. He cocked his one good ear "to the tune of the exhaust," and his one good eye was "glued to the tachometer."[93]

Wiley and Gatty spent just over three hours in Harbor Grace. They were 1,153 miles into the trip and had averaged an unbelievable 100 miles an hour, including the stop. At that rate, they could make it around the globe in seven days. Ahead was 1,900 miles of open ocean, with no railroad tracks, towns, or electric lines to provide hints of where they were. It was left to Harold Gatty to use his training and the predictable location of stars, sun and moon to plot the course. Gatty made a final reading on the setting sun as Wiley moved above the clouds for easier flying. Gatty remembered:

The moon came up as Wiley hung the ship on the propeller and barged upstairs. We came out at about 9,000 feet and caught up with the sun before it set behind us. We were above the cloud stratum which stretched before us and hid the ocean. Great mounds of cloud bulged menacingly above the mass ahead, so I worked fast while Wiley kept on climbing.[94]

Wiley tried different altitudes, trying to avoid the heavy "soup" they were flying through. It was a mammoth test of his "blind flying" skills. It was no use to look up or down, both the moon and the ocean were hidden by the clouds. When the ship trembled, Gatty was frightened.

The air speed took a sudden drop, and the compass "swung wide out to the right" while the liquid in it bounced around and the card tilted askew. It seemed as if the torque had taken hold of the ship and it was starting to get away from Wiley.

"Hey!" Gatty fairly screamed through the tube. He had heard about dropping out of the clouds in a spin.

"Hey, what?" Wiley's voice came back.

But by that time the indicator had returned to normal again, so Gatty merely said, "Oh, nothing. Just keep on dead ahead."

"Don't bother me with your damn directions now. Wait till we get out of this soup, and then I'll be tickled to death if you can tell us where we are," Wiley answered in his longest speech of the flight up to that time.[95]

Gatty made an entry in his logbook: "Flying blind."

The *Winnie Mae* flew steadily through the night, through sporadic rain storms and banks of puffy clouds. There was no sign of life below, no guide to their path. Gatty wanted to just open up the door and shout.

But Wiley plodded on—if you can call 150-miles-an-hour "plodding." He held the ship on an even keel and kept to his course. From the immovable indicators on his instruments the ship might just as well have been on the ground "with its tail resting up on a barrel." From time to time Gatty would give him directions, "A little more to the right, a little more to the left." [96]

Wiley had sold the exclusive rights to his reports of the flight to the *New York Times*. At the end of each leg, he cabled his report to New York upon landing. In the June 25, 1931 edition of the paper, Wiley wrote of the tense hours over the Atlantic:

> There is one thing I don't want to do right away again, and that is to fly the Atlantic. For three hours I could not see the engine at all and I just had to keep my eyes glued on the instruments. And it was only by the grace of God that we found that hole over Bangor in Wales, came down and found where we were.[97]

Wiley never had time to get hungry. He had a thermos bottle of tomato juice along, which he drained, and some cookies. He never touched the three sandwiches under his seat.

Wiley's daily reports appeared on the front page of the *New York Times* and in hundreds of other newspapers that had paid a fee to the North American Newspaper Association for the rights to reprint the articles. Often the *Times* provided a local reporter to take information from Wiley and put the story together. Wiley, always a blatantly honest fellow, never liked the idea of a "ghostwriter." One look at the daily dispatches from Wiley's trip shows which were written by Wiley and which by an experienced reporter. Wiley's language was down-to-earth and filled with Oklahoma references, the "ghostwriter's" efforts usually sounded poetic.

After 16 hours and 17 minutes Wiley saw an airport ahead and sat the *Winnie Mae* down at the Royal Air Force's Sealand Airdrome, ten miles from Liverpool, England. They had completed the twenty-eighth crossing of the Atlantic and had bested flying times of Charles Lindberg in 1927; Clarence Chamberlin and Charles Levine in 1927; Admiral Richard Byrd and three others in 1927; Amelia Earhart, Wilmer Stultz and Lou Gordon in 1928; and several other teams of pilots. Wiley and Gatty had won a laurel already, and they were only at the end of the first run.

Wiley was dog tired, "I was in too much of stupor to think or talk. The sound of the engine was still in my ears. When I opened my mouth to ask Gatty where we were, I couldn't hear the sound of my own voice. In a minute I heard the army officers surrounding the plane say we were in England. Before that, I had had no idea whether we had picked out Ireland, Scotland, or Wales. All I knew was that we had found land, and any land would have looked good as a place to set down."[98]

After a hearty meal of English roast beef, Wiley guided the *Winnie Mae* back into the English skies, opening up the Wasp to make up for the 80 minutes spent on the ground at Sealand.

Wiley picked up the Rhine River in the Netherlands and headed east to Berlin. He was tired and had trouble staying on course, "If we had been fresh and in trim, I don't suppose the country would have bothered us, but tired as we were, we just naturally roamed around a bit." From the canals and quaint houses of Holland they ran into the villages of Westphalia. About halfway to Berlin, Wiley picked up Hanover and made a landing there to get exact bearings and directions to the Tempelhof airdrome on the outskirts of Berlin.[99] At Hanover, Wiley and Gatty were so tired they forgot to check their fuel supply, taking for granted the promise of the Englishmen to put enough fuel in the tanks to get them to Berlin. After they took off from Hanover, they realized their fuel was short, so they landed again. It cost them 45 minutes.

Wiley was excited about landing for his first time at Tempelhof, built adjacent to the center of Berlin. He was impressed "with the nearness of the airport to the big squares in the town." He guessed when the Hohenzollern (the name of the ruling family of Prussia, the mightiest of German states) emperor ordered the imperial engineers to build a good parade ground, so the people would be inspired with the splendor of the nation, he didn't realize that he was building what would be the best airport of any large city in the world. Wiley thought, "Even out in roomy Oklahoma we can't seem to get the airports so close to town."[100]

Wiley circled the airport carefully and saw a huge crowd awaiting their arrival. All he wanted to do was slip away and find a place to sleep. But, the hospitable Germans would have nothing of that. The mob surrounded the airplane, dragged Wiley and Gatty out, and hoisted them to their collective shoulders. The Associated Press described the welcome:

Post and Gatty, "just passing through," on a round-the-world flight, received the most vociferous welcome tonight that Berlin has given any one for years. So enthusiastic was the crowd and so complicated were the police precautions to protect the fliers that Gatty was tangled up with the hero worshippers and was almost shouldered off the field by guards herding newspaper men and others away from the plane.[101]

It was a hero's welcome. The crowd began making noises in a language Wiley could not understand. A group of reporters surrounded him and fired questions at will. But when Wiley only mumbled a few words of English in reply, they soon "turned away disgustedly." Harold laughed aloud at Wiley's embarrassment. He had been in foreign countries before and knew what to do.[102]

New York Times reporter Kendal Foss wrote in a special report, on page one of the next day's edition of the paper, that the thousands gathered at the Berlin Airport had become excited every time a plane appeared on the horizon. Once, the band prematurely played "Stars and Stripes Forever" when a landing airplane was mistaken for the *Winnie Mae.*

Each time Wiley or Gatty spoke, the German crowd yelled, "Hoch!" Much to Wiley's surprise, a transatlantic radio broadcast had been set up. An announcer stuck a microphone in front of Wiley and told him to talk. Wiley obliged, "Hello, Germany and America!" Then the announcer asked, "How do you feel after your flight across the ocean?" Wiley simply stammered in his best parlor language, "Very good, so far, now that the worst is over."[103] Gatty spoke even more briefly, saying, "I haven't a thing to say."

German officials crowded around the Americans and escorted them to a lavish luncheon at the airport restaurant. Hundreds of curious onlookers hovered around the table and risked their lives by clinging to a perilous perch on the balcony of the eating establishment. Wiley startled the Germans by requesting ice water, even though there was plenty of champagne and German beer. He could see people nudge one another and grin as he drank. The cheering continued as many English, German, and American newspaper reporters questioned Wiley and Gatty.

Then Wiley cabled his daily report to the *New York Times:*

As soon as we got past the press photographers Herr Branden-
burg of the government aviation office took us into a little room
off the main restaurant in the airport hotel, where we found cold
meat, salad and a glass of port wine waiting. But I simply could
not resist asking for a glass of ice water. That was what I had been
longing for. Then I looked at the machine once more and
hopped for my bath and bed. . . . I am writing this in bed, so I
am afraid it can't be very much longer. For although I never felt
sleepiness while aloft, I feel it now all right.[104]

Before bed, the men talked to *Times* reporter Foss, who wrote:

After the last hangers-on had been shaken off, Post and Gatty
were taken to the airport's hotel, where they tumbled into a
steaming bath filled as high as possible, and while bathing drank
the lemonade which the hotel proprietor, having seen his strong
drinks scorned, had brought them. Post, telling his story to your
correspondent as he lay in the bath, continually dropped off to
sleep.[105]

The two-hour reception, and hours spent with reporters, wore
on the fliers. No bedtime stories or soft music were necessary for
Wiley and Gatty to drop into a deep, well-deserved sleep.

In Los Angeles, Vera Gatty heard the live broadcast from
Berlin. Tears welled in her gray eyes as she jumped up and down
with joy and turned the receiving set louder. When she heard Gatty's voice, she told her children, "That's him. Listen, your father is
talking from Berlin. Now isn't that just like him? He always was
bashful and never had more than a few words to say."[106]

In Oklahoma City, Wiley's brother James, an accountant, told
reporters the flight was "Wiley's show, not mine," but expressed
joy over the successful landing in Berlin. Mae, with friends in Walters, Oklahoma, said, "I knew they would do it. I think it's grand."

Near Maysville, Wiley's parents went about their work on the
farm "unworried and calmly." Younger son Arthur made occasional trips into town for the latest news of the flight.

FROM BERLIN TO RUSSIA

It was a rainstorm like a Kansas cloudburst—

W I L E Y   P O S T

FRESH from a desperately needed full night of sleep, Wiley and Gatty were anxious to lift off from Berlin and head toward Russia. The *Winnie Mae* had performed majestically, but Wiley knew some repairs and delays would be inevitable and he wanted to get as many miles behind him before something happened.

Wiley tried to pay the bill for gas and food, but as usual, some stranger picked up the tab. Gatty had spent the few dollars he brought with him on the trip. Wiley left New York with $34 and still had most of that meager amount. The fliers were so popular at every stop that someone always bought meals, paid for lodging, and purchased gasoline for the airplane at airports where previous arrangements for fuel had not been made by F. C. Hall and Wiley.

After Wiley warmed up the Wasp engine for ten to fifteen minutes to check out the Berlin-brand of aviation fuel that had filled the *Winnie Mae*, they took off from Berlin at 7:35 A.M., local time.

Wiley pulled back the stick and climbed rapidly until he reached the ceiling of 2,000 feet. There he flew "along the base of a dark cloud bank" which promised plenty of rain to Berlin within a short time. The air was muggy in the tightly closed cockpit and Wiley opened one of the windows on the right side.[107]

It was almost a thousand miles to Moscow, through Poland, East Prussia, and the burgeoning Russian state. In spite of their high rate of speed, Wiley could see the great contrast between the "quiet little domains of the Polish farmers," with their small homesteads and neat, but aged, clusters of outbuildings, and the "huge, rambling community centers of collective farming." Long barracks-like workers' houses and quantities of modern farm machinery were evidence of a wholesale production scheme.[108]

Communism was still relatively new and untried in Russia in 1931. Joseph Stalin had been in power for only seven years, and had instituted his first five-year plan for economic development only three years before. Collective farming and government control and ownership of land and production made up the cornerstone of Stalin's master plan.

Thirty minutes into Russia, the *Winnie Mae* encountered the worst weather so far on the trip. Wiley vividly described the storm:

> Five minutes later, 1 o'clock on the dash, it hit us! 'It' was a rainstorm like a Kansas cloudburst. I have never seen rain run so thick on a flying airplane. Usually it appears as a lot of little beads of water being blown along by the slipstream. Unless you look for them, you can hardly tell it is raining, except for the way the vision is dimmed. But that storm which burst right on the nose of the plane left no doubt that it was raining. It actually streamed along the cowling in front of me, and I could see clouds of steam coming out from under the ring around the engine, where the torrent was bouncing off the hot exhaust pipes.[109]

Wiley could hardly see past the propeller. "Blind flying" was worse over land than over the ocean. He said, "Hedgehopping through Russia with about 200 yards' visibility and 100 or more miles an hour speed is enough to make your hair stand on end every time you cross a fence."

The driving rain finally let up and Moscow was in sight. Wiley knew when they were getting near because he could see the railroads converging. He flew over the tracks until he was almost even with the city on his right, and then, "with a triumphant gesture," he banked around and headed southeast to circle the city before landing. It was still early, so he "tore around the old city twice to have a look at it." He and Gatty saw the old buildings and squares, the crooked, cobbled streets, and the newer outskirts built up since the Soviet regime.[110]

Gatty deliberately had plotted the course left of its intended destination. It was a crude, old navigational tool to take the guesswork out of making the proper turn when the time came. If all the errors of the day were on one side of the route, the landing point must be on the other side.

The landing in Moscow was the least spectacular of the trip. Only a handful of people, except for newspaper reporters, were on hand to greet Wiley and Gatty. Newspapers in Russia had scarcely mentioned the flight. Russian authorities approved their passports and transported the weary pilot and navigator into the center of Moscow in "a nice shiny American automobile."

The Savoy Hotel was better than Wiley anticipated, and the sight of a comfortable bed was too much of a temptation for him. Wiley "flopped right on it, clothes and all," and had to be forced to clean up for a formal nine-course dinner which had been arranged by the Society for Aviation and Chemical Defense.[111]

The lavish dinner thrown by the Russians lasted well into the night, until after 11 o'clock. Wiley and Gatty tried to act interested as toast after toast to their success was made. Wiley did not dare ingest even a small amount of alcohol that might impair his faculties during the trip, so he and Gatty drank water.

The *New York Times* reported on their condition:

Both men were in excellent condition, apparently unwearied by the flight of more than 900 miles from Berlin. When airdrome authorities expressed astonishment at the willingness of the airmen to attempt the difficult crossing of the Ural Mountains during the night, Post said with a broad Oklahoma drawl, 'Well, we flew over the ocean in the middle of the night in a hard storm. I don't expect the Urals to bother us much.'[112]

Wiley and Gatty were three days into the flight and had caught only a few hours of good sleep. The Savoy Hotel bed looked mighty good to them when the cheering Russians finally allowed them to retire for the night.[113]

Wiley and Gatty had trained themselves to eat light meals because of the fatigue factor on a heavy stomach and the practical problem of not having an available restroom in their cramped quarters. If the call of nature came during one of the long legs of the flight, they simply used a wax-coated ice cream carton and tossed it overboard.[114]

The Soviet organization that had sponsored the dinner in Moscow provided Gatty with up-to-date maps to assist on the flight to Novosibirsk, 2,600 miles and over 17 hours away.

The first major delay of the junket occurred in Moscow when the *Winnie Mae* was filled with imperial gallons of fuel, rather than U.S. gallons. The extra weight made it unsafe to take off from the Moscow airport. There was nothing to do but take some of the gas out of the tanks.

Wiley wanted to bleed it out through the line at the bottom of the tank, but airport officials feared the fire hazard if so much fuel was dumped on the ground. A mechanic started to siphon gas from one of the tanks. The precious minutes wore on. Wiley knew that if he did not "get away quickly," he would have to finish the flight in darkness.

Time after time the mechanic lost the suction on the siphon. Still muttering, Wiley watched them, "admonishing the workers in no uncertain tones." Of course they couldn't understand a word he said, but two or three times the young woman who was acting as interpreter "blushed and changed her translations a little."[115]

Wiley and Gatty soon took over the siphoning job and brought the fuel level down sufficiently to ensure a safe takeoff from the rough Moscow runway. Wiley was upset by the delay. By 4:30 A.M. everything was ready to go.

The Wasp "caught" on the first pull, and roared loudly. The staccato notes of the exhausts dispelled all of Wiley's impetuous mood. The last of his fretting was "blown back by the propeller wash" and he was once more the efficient and tranquil pilot, businesslike and patient. "Let's go kid," he shouted above the swish of the idling air screw.[116]

Wiley headed down the runway like a man on the way to a fire. He pointed *Winnie Mae's* nose into the northwest wind, as Gatty sat quietly:

> And was that field bumpy? Well, two or three times on that run of less than 300 yards, before we bounced into the air, I fully expected the struts on the landing gear to come up through the cabin. We were first on one wheel, then on the other. Wiley had his hands full keeping the thing straight at our 70-mile speed.[117]

Wiley headed for altitude and "poured the soup" to the engine. "Like a frightened colt, *Winnie Mae* increased her usual steady lope to a wild gallop, as she ripped a hole through the Soviet air."

On went the Americans, across the Oka River, the Volga River, to Kazan, and the Ural Mountains. They followed a railroad to Chelyabinsk and Kurgan and then followed Gatty's meticulous flight plan to Omsk, the largest town on the line to Novosibirsk.

They picked up a tail wind and averaged 176 miles an hour for much of the leg, making it to Novosibirsk 90 minutes early. Novosibirsk was a new Soviet city on the River Ob, a city that had been built originally by the workers who constructed a railroad to Manchuria.

The female interpreter at Moscow had written out, in Russian, several blank forms for Wiley to use to communicate his instructions on fueling and maintaining the *Winnie Mae*. The forms worked and soon the plane was topped off and ready to fly again the next dawn. Wiley and Gatty were escorted like visiting dignitaries to the city. Large crowds followed them through the narrow streets to an ancient hotel where they trudged up "a somber staircase" to the fifth floor.

Hot, or even running water, was one of the unknown mysteries in the hotel but they did get a chance to sponge themselves in the public bath, where the water dropped from a big tank into a tin basin with a "slow, maddening trickle." Wiley and Gatty were just about ready to snatch some sleep when their host invaded their sanctum, "two hard beds with blankets and no linen," and almost forcibly escorted them to the head of the stairs. It seemed that they had another banquet coming.[118]

They trekked through the streets to a restaurant to a meal fit for a king. Gatty said if he was ever really hungry, he would go back to Novosibirsk. He called his steak "the acme of perfection."

Even Wiley began to take some interest in the banquet. The hours sped by without waiting for the tired fliers, and it was ten o'clock before they realized it. When they explained to the "buxom" woman who was interpreting that they had only about three hours for sleep before a 20-hour flight to Khabarovsk, she hurried them out to the hotel.[119]

Wiley slumped onto the hard bed in his clothes, yanked the blanket up over his chin, and passed out. Gatty had problems with bedbugs and woke up with welts all over his face.

Wiley and Gatty had to share headlines in the *New York Times* on June 27, 1931, with Captain Holger Horiss and Otto Hillig, two aviators who took off a few hours after the *Winnie Mae* from New York's Roosevelt Field. Horiss and Hillig had finally made it to Horiss' homeland of Denmark where he was knighted by King Christian. One hundred thousand people jammed the Copenhagen airport as Horiss and Hillig's plane, the *Liberty*, landed.

As the *Liberty* "swooped toward the ground at the airport" the crowd broke through the barriers and ran toward the plane. After a champagne toast of welcome the fliers entered waiting automobiles and began "a long triumphal journey" through all the main thoroughfares of Copenhagen. The streets were lined by enormous crowds in summer garb and in summer spirits, ready to give rousing cheers as the procession passed. Streams were hung from the upper stories of most houses and showers of confetti rained down. Girls crowded the windows of every floor of department stores, waving to the airmen and releasing thousands of toy balloons which "rose toward the blue sky in a riot of colors."[120]

SIBERIA

His clothes stuck to him in queer folds—

H A R O L D   G A T T Y

IBERIA is a vast region comprising the eastern part of Russia, bounded on the west by the Ural Mountains; on the north by the Arctic Ocean; on the east by the Pacific Ocean; and on the south by China and Mongolia.

In developing a flight plan, Wiley avoided the frozen, sparsely populated tundra in northern Siberia, opting instead to fly across southern Siberia which was dotted with population centers, mountains, and dense forests.

At Novosibirsk, Wiley and Gatty were smack dab in the middle of Siberia. After the incredible banquet the night before, the Americans awoke at 1:00 A.M. and quickly exited the hotel and caught a ride to the airport. It was "traveling light" for Wiley and Gatty because they had no luggage. With three hours sleep under their belts, they took off.

They "ripped the air wide open" across the railhead at Novosibirsk. In just a few minutes there was nothing in the world that mattered to Wiley but "good old *Winnie Mae* and her trusty motor, Gatty, and a few scrubby fields." Wiley held the compass at 70 degrees and climbed to 4,000 feet.[121]

Wiley was able to navigate over the tracks of the Trans-Siberian railroad for the next three hours, allowing Gatty to take a nap. It gave time for Wiley to reflect on his buddy in the back seat:

Gatty was a good passenger, one of the best I ever carried. He never asked any questions or raised any disturbance about the way I pulled that ship up or knocked it down in dives that I know must have plugged his ears.[122]

Wiley woke Gatty up when clouds began to form at 4,000 feet. It began to rain. The air suddenly grew "rough and gusty." Just as quickly it became smooth again as the rain pelted the airplane in sheets. The air behind the 450-horsepower motor was like the steam room of a Turkish bath. Wiley was soaking wet.[123]

Wiley assumed the town he saw ahead was Irkutsk, because they had passed only a few isolated cities along the way. He had never heard of any cities in those parts except Irkutsk, of course he had never heard of Irkutsk until he planned the trip around the world.

It was strange country Wiley and Gatty were flying over. At Irkutsk, "standing at the influx of the Irkut River into the Angara," about 30 miles from the northwesterly shore of Lake Baikal, they saw one of the larger Siberian cities with a strong accent of the Orient.

For all its "stone houses, its noted geographical society and its magnetic-meteorological observatory," it was a market city for the wares of the East. Tea, rhubarb, fruits and Chinese products passed through the city on its way to customers in Western Russia. They passed over Chita and saw beneath them the seemingly never-ending woods that merge into the gold-mining region which surrounds Blagoveshchensk, whose Russia name means "annunciation."[124]

The largest crowd since Berlin met Wiley and Gatty as they landed at Irkutsk. Wiley liked the people of Eastern Russia:

Those Russians in the western sections of the USSR are industrious people and have no time for the "tomfoolery" of a pair of flyers. But Irkutsk is a Russia of the older regime. The folks there have leisure, and a few hours wasted at the airport makes little difference in the long run of their lives.[125]

Wiley sent only a brief cable to the *New York Times*, "We are now half way around the world in three days and twenty hours. Our physical condition is perfect and we are continuing immediately for Blagoveshchensk."[126]

With the help of a 16-year-old girl, Annie Polikof, who had lived as a child in England, Wiley sent a two-word cable to his wife. It said, "feeling fine." It was the middle of the afternoon and Wiley wanted to get farther east before nightfall. They were on the ground at Irkutsk only two hours.

Wiley hopped in and "got the engine going" while Gatty signed a couple of souvenirs for Annie. Wiley waved good-bye to the crowd and started taxiing out as Gatty jumped into his seat and closed the door. "In a whirl of dust and flying bits of grass," the *Winnie Mae* streaked across another rough Soviet runway and was on her way.[127]

Soon the *Winnie Mae* flew over the tip of Manchuria, where nomads roamed for centuries. For two hours there was no sign of life below. When Wiley crossed the 3,000-mile Amur River that formed part of the border between Russia and China, he had his work cut out for him.

Just as it gets light in Siberia early in the morning, Wiley found that darkness sets in early. It came "swiftly and without warning of a long twilight." To make matters worse, it had been raining all day in Blagoveshchensk, and the sky was still overcast. Wiley saw the town but could not locate the airport, which was supposed to have been marked by oil flares.[128]

Wiley finally spotted the lights of the airport. In the rain, the flares looked like they were setting on top of a lake. Wiley slid in over the river and cut the engine. Night landings had never bothered him before, but all the lights he had merely gave "an outline of a rectangle." There was not much Wiley could do but feel his way to the ground and trust his luck.[129]

Wiley tried to land on one of the few semi-dry spots on the airfield. He thought they were in a seaplane. Spray flew all over the place. Mud clogged up the pants on the wheels. Almost as the plane touched, Wiley felt "that oozy mud." No bounce, no run.

They rolled less than 400 feet at a speed close to 80 miles an hour. As long as the ship kept moving, they were all right, but Wiley could not keep her going. She got "heavier and heavier," and when he tried to turn, he felt her left wheel sink.[130]

Wiley's heart sank with that wheel! Was this the end of a so-far perfect flight, in a mudhole in the last 300 miles of Siberia?

A few people waded the mud in hipboots to meet the plane. Wiley and Gatty used a rope tied to an old Ford, driven by two Danish telegraph operators, to try to pull the *Winnie Mae* from the mire and muck. The wheels of the car spun helplessly, tossing out "a black fountain." The airplane dug herself deeper in the bog.

Wiley and Gatty shouted, raved, and ranted. At last one of the airport officials announced that he had sent for a tractor. He suggested that the American airmen go into town and sleep, and said that he would have a gang of laborers with the tractor there by morning to get the plane out.

Gatty was wet to the skin and covered with slime. After much persuasion he decided to abandon the ship for the time being.[131]

Gatty looked for any comic relief to defuse the moment:

> When I looked at Wiley, I just had to give way to my feelings. I was bedraggled myself, but I doubt if anyone ever looked as funny as he did then. He waddled into the lighted room, dragging one foot behind the other. His clothes stuck to him in queer folds. His face was spattered with mud, and he wore that dejected look of comic pathos with which Charlie Chaplin established the reputation that brought him fame and fortune.[132]

Wiley decided to stay with his airplane and wait for the farm tractor to arrive. He fell asleep in Gatty's navigator chair. Meanwhile, Gatty accepted an invitation from the Danish telegraph operators to dine with them. First, however, Gatty took his first real hot tub bath since New York, and then ate a healthy Danish dinner of sausages and coffee. When he arrived back at the airfield, Wiley was still asleep in the plane.

Wiley prodded a nearby Siberian farmer to bring his plow horses to attempt to dislodge the airplane. The promised tractor had still not arrived at daylight so the horses provided the last chance to get out of Siberia. The rain had stopped and the ground dried up enough to give the animals a good foothold. With the combined pulling power of the horses and a dozen men with ropes, the *Winnie Mae* came out with "a great heave." They had lost 12 hours in Blagoveshchensk.

It was an uneventful flight of less than 400 miles to Khabarovsk, the last stop in Russia. Khabarovsk, on the border between Russia and China, lay at the junction of the Amur and the Ussuri Rivers, where the Ussuri branch of the Trans-Siberian railroad left the main tracks. Khabarovsk was 400 miles north of Vladivostok, about 200 miles inland from the Siberian coast.

Wiley and Gatty had plenty of time to think about their next, and most difficult leg, a 2,441-mile jaunt from Khabarovsk to Solomon, Alaska, a "route fraught with the difficulties of over-water flying, fog, and unknown mountains."

Wiley took extra precautions during the stop at Khabarovsk to make certain the *Winnie Mae* was in good working order. The plane had received even less care than the fliers since she had "spanked her wing against the wet air at Roosevelt Field 5½ days before." Wiley knew his ship needed attention, "Pilots may fly when they have rheumatism, navigators may guide without maps, but unless airplanes are given a certain amount of personal attention, they will become perverse." Wiley began by going to work on "the old girl's heart." He was certain that there was something he could do to improve her condition and to reassure her that her days of hard work were about at an end.[133]

Wiley changed out four spark plugs on the Wasp engine while Gatty collected weather data and pored over his charts and maps, seeking the shortest and best route to Alaska. Badly in need of sleep, and waiting on more information about a storm in the Sea of Japan, Wiley and Gatty headed for the hotel. In three hours they arrived back at the airfield. The wind was blowing straight across the runway so there was no way the *Winnie Mae* could take off with a full load of fuel. They were not too disappointed because they were so sleepy.

They went into one of the hangars and stretched out on a couple of cots and dropped off to sleep. They both slept until the next afternoon. When they awoke, wind conditions had changed enough to make the takeoff with a full load possible.[134]

The Americans headed up the Amur River, flying just 75 feet off the water in order to make better time against a slight head wind. The noisy drone of the airplane frightened natives paddling in their sampans. The sight and sound of the *Winnie Mae* must have been terrifying to them in "that last few minutes of daylight." It probably was the first time they had ever seen an airplane.[135]

It was decision time. Should they try to go over the Great Circle Route directly to Solomon, Alaska, or should they fly due east for the lower tip of the Kamchatka Peninsula and refuel at Petropavlovsk? After calculating their speed, now at just 140 miles an hour, they decided they had enough fuel and the weather was good enough to try another 18 hours in the air, to that point in history, man's longest flight.

The *Winnie Mae* was now out over water again. Wiley wrote:

The weather began to grow thicker every minute as we tore across that sea in the darkest hours of the moonless night. By the time we were out over the middle of it, at 150 degrees E. Longitude, I was forced down to within a few feet of the water. A few bumps warned me that side gusts were hitting the wing. The gusts were so violent that I might have been flying through a mountain pass like some I had run across, which actually threw the ship momentarily out of control. But I knew there was nothing except water underneath.[136]

Wiley grew tired of dodging sea waves and decided to "go upstairs" and fly blind. He relaxed, kept his eyes on his instruments, and "felt" his way through the choppy skies. He slid his window back to get some fresh air, thrust his hand out, and quickly brought it back. It was hailing, which Wiley said "cut like shot" as the plane zipped away into the night at 155 miles an hour.

Suddenly the hail changed to rain. Wiley could see nothing else outside. He had flown through tropical showers on the mail runs in Mexico and thought they might be described as the heaviest waterfalls in the world. But this rain over the Sea of Okhotsk was so heavy that it reminded him of a joke about the pilot who was flying an amphibian through the rain. The pilot said he had noticed some funny-looking lumps gathering on the wing, had reached out, and had pulled in a fish.[137]

Every few hours Wiley pulled above the clouds to give Gatty a chance to use the stars and the moon to figure out where they were. Their Russian maps were anything but accurate in regard to heights of mountains, and more than once, Wiley had to put the *Winnie Mae* into rapid climbs to avoid mountains that were obviously higher than indicated on the maps.

Sometime in the middle of Tuesday, June 30, the *Winnie Mae* crossed the International Date Line on the 180th Meridian. It was now the middle of Monday, June 29. For the first time in his life Wiley had a chance to live a day over again. He thought, " If I were given all my former days to relive, I should never devote any hours of them to duplicating the three hours which followed. Fog, rain, fog, and more rain. We thundered through the mist and drizzle. I would gladly have swapped that day's gain on Old Man Time for an hour, or even a few minutes, of direct sunlight."[138]

The weather broke briefly over St. Lawrence Island and Gatty took a bearing. He felt better about being in a part of the world where the maps were more reliable. The fog closed in again. It was a two-hour flight to Solomon, and only two hours of fuel remained on board. The *Winnie Mae* leveled off at 6,000 feet.[139]

Finally, Fort Davis and Solomon, Alaska came into view. Somehow, Gatty had navigated, and Wiley had flown, almost a full earth's day in a tiny airplane over uncharted mountains and waters. Wiley landed his beloved *Winnie Mae* on a beach. As they touched, the tail rose a little as the deep sand swirled up around the pants of the wheels. The sandy beach made a natural, though unreliable, brake. At last the ship stopped, and the idling motor throbbed "like a tired runner."[140]

HOMEWARD BOUND

We're a little bit tired of sittin' down—

W I L E Y   P O S T

I T W A S O N L Y 2 : 4 5 in the afternoon when Wiley sat the *Winnie Mae* down on the beach at Solomon, a trading post and native village 36 miles east of Nome on Alaska's Seward Peninsula. Wiley was glad to be back on American soil. His report to the *New York Times* was brief, "Sixteen hours in the plane over water and No Man's Land is enough for us, but it's colder than a son of gun up here. We had great trouble in getting the food we are accustomed to all through Siberia. Rye bread was practically all we ate."[141]

If Wiley could refuel quickly, they could make Fairbanks by dark. With 100 gallons of fuel aboard, he taxied along the beach. Suddenly the ship started to sink into the sand. With a quick thrust Wiley "banged the throttle open" to pull her through it before they were stuck. But all he did was to boost the tail up into the air. "With a loud slap" the propeller cut a hole in the sand and bent both tips on the blades. Wiley cut the emergency switch just in time to keep the *Winnie Mae* "from making an exhibition of herself by standing on her nose." That would have been fatal to his hopes.[142]

Wiley jumped out of the plane and used a wrench, a broken-handled hammer, and a round rock to straighten out the tips so "they would at least fan the air in the right direction." Gatty swung the prop to restart the hot engine. He called out "all clear" and Wiley yanked the switch.

One of the hot charges of gasoline caught on the upstroke of the piston, and with a back fire the Wasp kicked. The propeller flew out of Gatty's hands, and one of the blades smacked his shoulder "before he could jump clear of the track." He dropped like a log. It was the flat side of the blade that hit him. If the prop had been going the other way, "he might have been sliced in two."[143]

Gatty's only injuries were a wrenched back and arm and a bruised ego. He recovered his senses and on he and Wiley flew to Fairbanks. It took them less than four hours to cover the 510 miles, where they turned the *Winnie Mae* over to crack mechanics at Alaskan Airways.

Not only did they "wipe her down, refuel, and oil her," but they had a gleaming new propeller just the right size. The fliers' spirits were much better when they left the landing field for a short three or four hours of sleep at the local hotel. Wiley closed his eyes and thought:

> Our trip was nearly over. Success was within our grasp. When
> we turned out the light. . . , we both agreed that nothing short
> of fire, earthquake, or some other unforeseen catastrophe
> beyond the control of the firm of Post, Gatty and Co., could
> stop us from setting a record which should withstand the
> snipers and sharpshooters of aviation for some time to come.[144]

Wiley and Gatty were only 3,000 miles from New York and a new world's record. The nation was getting excited about the trip. The *New York Times* continued to cover the flight in the most prominent position of its front page, complete with maps showing the progress of the trip, and reactions from about anyone who would give a reaction. NBC news reporter Charles Lyons left his post in Chicago and flew to Edmonton, Alberta, Canada, where the network planned to carry the arrival live.

Wiley and Gatty slept most of the six hours they were on the ground in Fairbanks. They were refreshed as "the Lockheed poked her white prow and new prop up over the mountains."

They caught a good tail wind and crossed the Canadian border within 90 minutes of Fairbanks. They swung east over the Klondike country, Dawson, and into the Canadian Rockies. Hardly a word passed between Wiley and Gatty, they were content to sit quietly and absorb "the vitality generated by the crisp air."

Both men were thinking about New York, expected crowds, and a new record. Gatty was depressed for a moment and lost his enthusiasm for the trip. He asked himself, "Who cares? Is it worth this nerve-wracking dive through the rain, or putting my family through the worry I know they must be having? The loneliness of the country was beginning to upset my mental equilibrium. I tried to whistle, but the engine drowned out any amusement... Good old Wiley! He just sat up there and flew."[145]

When the *Winnie Mae* broke through the clouds, the first thing Wiley saw was the Canadian National Railway branch that runs west from Edmonton to Prince Rupert, British Colombia. The track was a "godsend, a sort of sop for rain." They ripped off the miles over the tracks "like a crack express," with only the click of the wheels across the rail joints missing. Where the railroad widened into the yards, they picked up a high bluff with the Hotel MacDonald on top. "Edmonton—all out!" Wiley shouted.[146]

Another big crowd waited patiently in the rain as Wiley literally flew the airplane through the mud up to the hangar apron. He wasn't about to slow down and get stuck again. The crowd broke through the police lines and crowded around the *Winnie Mae*. Reporters, photographers, and radio announcers all vied for Wiley's attention. Gatty observed:

Wiley was so tired, so disheartened, and so apprehensive on account of the mud-soaked condition of the field that he made two or three bitter remarks under his breath, which fortunately were unnoticed by the hospitable Canadians. In the turmoil somebody held a microphone up in front of him, but all he could think of saying was that he was tired of sitting down.[147]

Wiley was disheartened because it could be days before the mud on the runway was dry and solid enough to take off from. A Canadian airmail pilot suggested that Portage Avenue, a straight two-mile street that ran from the airport to downtown Edmonton, be turned into a runway. Wiley surveyed the street and agreed. Local officials ordered emergency crews to take down electric wires along the street to clear the way for takeoff the next morning.

Wiley and Gatty were met at the hotel by a flood of telegrams and mail. They were back to civilization, and the telephone. Gatty said he would sooner fly the Bering Sea again than "face a bunch of photographers pleading for 'just one more.'" Newspapers and well-wishers from all over America tried to get through to their hotel but their hosts protected them from most of the disturbances, allowing them to go to bed early.

NBC reporter Charles Lyons interviewed Wiley and Gatty live upon their arrival in Edmonton. Through tired eyes and frail voice Wiley said, "We're very glad to be so near home—at least back where people can speak our language and we don't have to make signs for everything. . . and where we don't have to eat black bread all the time. . . We're a little bit tired of sitting down."[148]

Back in New York City, newspapers clamored for any angle on the biggest story of the day. A reporter found F. C. Hall and Mae shopping:

> Mr. Hall, a man of medium height, with eyes that snap when he talks, explained that Post. . . had 'promoted' him into sponsoring the flight. He had 'sunk' about $100,000 in aviation, he said, as the backer of two endurance flights 'that didn't come off very well,' and the most recent venture, which did.
>
> Mrs. Post, before her shopping expedition started, told. . . it is a strain to follow the course of a husband around the world for eight days and there was at least one sleepless night while the Winnie Mae was fighting the North Atlantic on its way to England. . .

Replying to a question regarding her attitude the 'next time,' if there should be one, she smiled and said in her Southwestern drawl: 'Well, I wouldn't exactly want to do it, but if he insisted I suppose I'd tell him to go ahead.' Mrs. Post, who has been married four years and is only 21 now, shares with Mr. Hall the belief that her husband is the 'greatest pilot in the world.' [149]

All of Edmonton turned out at the airport the next morning to see Wiley and Gatty off. The mud had been washed from the *Winnie Mae*, described by Gatty that day as "a little girl all ready to be a flower girl at a wedding."

As Wiley warmed up the engine, the rain stopped. Canadian mounted policemen cleared the traffic from Portage Avenue. A throng of people crowded dangerously close to the airplane as Wiley "revved" the engine up one last time before letting go of the brakes.

The ship hurtled down that street. Curbstones and electric-light poles clipped by the wing tips so fast that Wiley was "just a little scared." The wind was slightly across their path, and if one wing had ever dropped, it would have been just too bad. Within 15 seconds the outlying houses of town had dropped under the nose. By the time they reached the first turn in the street, they were 500 feet above the pavement. As Wiley flew over the Hotel MacDonald, where their late maitre d' was "out on the roof with his whole army of bellhops in array" to salute them going by, the ground dropped away fast, and they turned over the high bluff where the hotel sat.[150]

A few hours later, the *Winnie Mae* entered its home country, the United States of America, just north of Bessemer Junction, Michigan. Wiley shouted back to Gatty, "How does this look to you?" Gatty replied, "Didn't see any country I liked better on the whole trip."

The flight of the *Winnie Mae* was the most important thing happening in the whole world on July 1, 1931. Americans gathered around their radios to hear updates on the flight. A huge crowd of 5,000 gave Wiley and Gatty a rousing welcome as they stopped to refuel at Municipal Airport in Cleveland, Ohio. Some admiring fan even tore the pocket off Gatty's coat. NBC asked aviator Elinor Smith to interview Wiley and Gatty in Cleveland. As usual the boys had little to say. Gatty told his wife and children he badly wanted to see them and talked about the differences between him and Wiley, "We have a little trouble understanding each other. The trouble is I speak English and Wiley speaks Oklahoman."

Under a scorching sun at Cleveland, Wiley and Gatty anxiously awaited the refueling of their plane. Just a half hour after arriving, and 192 gallons of gasoline later, they boarded the *Winnie Mae* and sped down the runway.

Only one stop left... New York... New York. Wiley later recalled, "Then came the biggest thrill of my life—the New York sky line. What a sight! We had gone all the way around the world for a glimpse of it from the west!"[151]

The air around Roosevelt Field was filled with airplanes, all carrying photographers hoping for an exclusive shot of the *Winnie Mae*'s triumphant return to New York. Wiley made an extra turn around the airport, much to the delight of the salivating photographers on the ground.

Wiley came in high over the hangars and the gigantic crowd, and slipped the *Winnie Mae* down on the hard-surfaced runway. Wiley yelled back at Gatty, "Well, here we are, kid."

Walter D. Ward, the official timer of the National Aeronautic Association, computed and announced the official time—eight days, 15 hours, 51 minutes, by far a new world record. The "two young men in a hurry," as one newspaper called them, had flown 15,474 miles in just under 208 hours. The actual flying time was 107 hours and two minutes, averaging a phenomenal 146 miles an hour.

Wiley Post and Harold Gatty had successfully completed their dream—AROUND THE WORLD IN EIGHT DAYS!

New York City honored Wiley and Gatty with a ticker-tape parade on July 2, 1931. It was the largest parade in the city's history, surpassing the welcome given Charles Lindbergh and Admiral Richard Byrd. Courtesy Oklahoma Historical Society.

A HERO'S WELCOME

I knew the boys could do it—

F. C. HALL

THERE WAS ABSOLUTE PANDEMONIUM (and that is a terrible literary understatement) at Roosevelt Field as Wiley taxied the *Winnie Mae* from the runway. Ten thousand people scaled fences and broke through police lines to get close to the airplane. A newspaper account of the event read like fiction:

> What promised to be one of the most orderly receptions approached a riot tonight when Wiley Post and Harold Gatty landed on the field from which they had arisen only nine days ago, having completed the circuit of the world.
>
> As thirty motorcycles, ridden by Nassau County policemen, who had gone out on the field to meet the plane, plowed into the oncoming throng, scores of flashlights popped and flashed, women screamed, and, in their efforts to protect the two aviators, many of the 300 patrolmen on duty shoved and clubbed those nearest at hand, heightening the confusion. Many were bruised in the struggle.[152]

New York Times reporter F. Raymond Danieli described the end of the flight as "the fastest trip ever made by man around the earth on which he lives." Danieli called the flight a success when Wiley "brought the cream-white monoplane to earth at sundown in a cloud of dust... with the speed of a meteor as the sinking sun turned the cloud-flocked blue sky to a brilliant pink backdrop."[153]

On July 1, 1931, ten thousand people broke through police lines at New York's Roosevelt Field to greet Wiley and Gatty as they hopped out of the *Winnie Mae* after their around-the-world trip. The weariness of the pilot and his navigator shows on their faces. Wiley had slept only 15 hours in the previous eight days. Their shoes and pants are splattered with oil from doing much of their own maintenance on the plane. Courtesy *The Daily Oklahoman*.

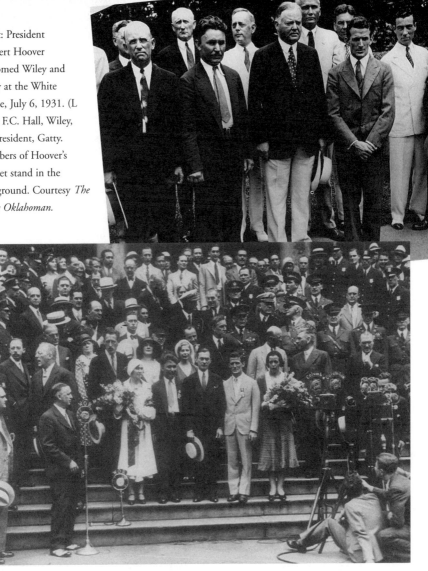

Right: President Herbert Hoover welcomed Wiley and Gatty at the White House, July 6, 1931. (L to R) F.C. Hall, Wiley, the President, Gatty. Members of Hoover's cabinet stand in the background. Courtesy *The Daily Oklahoman.*

Above: New York City Mayor James J. Walker poses with Wiley, Gatty, and their wives on the steps of City Hall after the ticker-tape parade up Broadway past cheering thousands. Walker told the crowd that Wiley and Gatty were "the most fearless men in history." Newsreel cameras and radio microphones recorded the event. Courtesy Oklahoma Historical Society.

Facing: The Aeronautical Chamber of Commerce presented Wiley (right) and Gatty with bronze plaques, commemorating their around-the-world flight in 1931. Courtesy Oklahoma Historical Society.

When Wiley finally throttled back the *Winnie Mae*'s engine and stopped, the crowd converged on the airplane. Wiley, "his cheeks hollowed by fatigue, his face an ashen gray," leaped to the ground. His knees sagged and the police had to use their clubs to protect him from the enthusiastic crowd. Within a radius of 40 feet the scene "resembled several football scrimmages proceeding at once." Loud cheers and a bombardment of flashes from photographers' cameras accompanied radio men diving madly through their entangled wires to get a glimpse of the fliers.

Mae Post was almost hysterical as she was escorted by two six-foot policemen out to the plane. She and Wiley had been separated for six weeks and she fought back tears as she greeted her husband with a smile.

Gatty somehow pulled his tired body from the plane and just sat on the wing. Unfortunately, his wife Vera had missed the moment because her plane from California had been forced by bad weather to land in Pittsburgh. It would still be another day before she could get to New York for the festivities.

F. C. Hall tried to remain cool, calm, and collected as the *Winnie Mae* arrived home safely. Up to the moment of the arrival, Hall had retained his poise, the only sign of nervous strain a flexing of the jaw muscles. Clutching to his straw hat to keep the maddened throng from crushing it, he saw the plane and exclaimed, "Lord, what a demonstration! What a demonstration!" A newspaper reporter overheard Hall mutter under his breath, "Damn! I didn't expect to see that plane ever again." A second later he apologized and said, "Shouldn't say that, I guess." Hall was clearly overcome by emotion and kept saying, "I knew the boys could do it, I knew the boys could do it."[154]

Police cleared a path for a waiting automobile to whisk Wiley and Gatty to a nearby hangar where broadcast microphones were set up. The nation waited for the newest American heroes to tell about the trip. About all Wiley would say at first was, "Well, we had a good time." The one-eyed pilot from Oklahoma wasn't much of a speaker, but he was a whale of a pilot. F. C. Hall told the nationwide NBC hookup:

Hello, Oklahoma! This is the most wonderful demonstration I have ever seen, honoring Mr. Post, Mr. Gatty, their families and my family, and my little girl in Long Beach, California. We will be in Chickasha in four or five days. Goodbye.[155]

Broadcasting, like aviation, was still in its infant stages in America and the world. The Post-Gatty flight was an important milestone in radio's "coming of age." The entire country was able to experience the thrill of being at the finish line as the epoch flight ended at Roosevelt Field. Coast-to-coast networks in the United States and shortwave stations in foreign countries broadcast the "play-by-play" description of the landing. Graham McNamee and Floyd Gibbons, prominent national announcers, manned two of the four NBC microphones placed in strategic locations around Roosevelt Field.

Among the 10,000 on hand at the airport to greet Wiley and Gatty were Major Jimmy Doolittle and Charles Lindbergh, who tried to sneak past the gatekeeper as "just one of the crowd."[156]

A bold headline greeted readers of the *New York Times* on the morning of July 2, 1931: POST AND GATTY END THEIR RECORD WORLD FLIGHT; CIRCLE GLOBE IN 8 DAYS, 15 HOURS, 51 MINUTES

In less than three years, Wiley Post had been transformed from an unknown barnstormer to the world's most famous pilot, and the next few days proved it. Newspapers around the world, from New York to Maysville, Oklahoma ran banner headlines about the trip. The *Times,* that had run daily stories before, and during the trip, devoted much of its front page and several inside pages to coverage of the flight. Several editorials in the *Times* praised the accomplishments of the two young fliers. The paper called the flight "a test of men, fabric, and engine":

It was if messengers had come out of the skies to the earthdwellers with promise of greater victories, for man has not yet come to the limit of his striving with the forces of sea and air and land.[157]

The Daily Oklahoman editorialized that Wiley's flight had given Americans new confidence in the safety of flying:

> Such feats as that of Post and Gatty are destined to become commonplace before the world is very much older. Ere long, the world will pay no more attention to the feat cheered so insanely at Roosevelt Field Wednesday than it will to a morning flight from New York to Philadelphia. The future of the human race is in the air.[158]

The *Oklahoman* praised the wives of Wiley and Gatty for encouraging their husbands to undertake what the paper called "one of the greatest adventures in history."[159]

Most important political and aviation leaders had something to say about the flight. Rear Admiral William A. Moffett, chief of the Naval Branch of Aeronautics, said the flight "cannot but assure the public of the reliability of aircraft." Assistant Navy Secretary David Ingalls said the flight was not only a tribute to the reliability of aircraft but also "an extraordinary tribute to the ability, fortitude and endurance of Wiley and Harold."

Assistant Secretary of War Trubee Davison said, "Because of you the world is smaller than ever before." Pratt and Whiney Aircraft Corporation president Don L. Brown was a prophet, "They have shown the way, which, in years to come, may possibly result in the inauguration of regular air transportation from country to country, eventually encircling the globe." World-famous fliers Clarence Chamberlin, Clyde Pangborn and Hugh Herndon called the flight "the most spectacular in aviation to date."

World leaders praised the accomplishments of Wiley and Gatty. The head of Germany's Lufthansa issued a statement calling the flight "a great achievement." Australian flier Charles Kingsford-Smith, conquerer of two oceans, described the exploits as "one of the greatest feats of endurance." Foreign newspapers heralded the trip. In London, the *Daily Telegraphic* called it a "nine days' wonder." The *London Mirror* said, "Their pluck, endurance and cheeriness must always be remembered in the story of the flight." A

French newspaper headlined the story with the bold statement, "We bow down before this fantastic performance which seems to belong yet to the kingdom of dreams."

An article in the *New York Times* proved just how "big" the flight had been in America:

> Spanning more than half the continent on the last day of their dash around the world, Post and Gatty were followed in spirit by millions of Americans yesterday as they sped from Edmonton to Roosevelt Field. From lonely wheat farms in the great grain areas of the Northwest to the smoky, industrial East, the skies were scanned by millions for a brief sight of the white-winged plane, and those whose fortune it was to catch a brief glimpse of the plane passed the word to myriads of others, equally fascinated by the brilliant flight. . .
>
> Villages and cities alike rejoiced in the brief distinction of identifying themselves with the path of the record-breakers, as they made known to the nation that the trim white monoplane had passed overhead.[160]

In New York, Wiley and Gatty were heroes of the highest order. Wiley later wrote, "All I know of the next few days is a muddle. We were wined and dined until the very sight of food made me shudder. I even remember wishing that I had cracked up on the last landing. Then, at least, I would have had a nice reclining ride in an ambulance to some quiet hospital, where my dream of sleep would have been realized."[161]

Thousands were waiting at the Ritz-Carlton Hotel when Wiley and Mae arrived. Many in the crowd had been unable to travel to Roosevelt Field and had waited for hours to see the fliers. Wiley and Mae were taken to a fourth floor suite where an army of photographers and reporters met them. Fortunately, the interview in the hallway was cut short when Wiley was informed that New York mayor Jimmy Walker was on the telephone.

Wiley and Gatty received the ultimate in a hero's welcome, a ticker-tape parade down Broadway in New York. It was the largest turnout in the city's history, larger than the parade for Lindbergh or Admiral Byrd, a tribute to the Oklahoma pilot who had overcome tremendous odds to charm the world about the future of aviation.

The *New York Times* said the parade left Wiley and Gatty "a little dizzy but very happy." Ten thousand people gathered at Battery Park, the beginning point of the parade, hours before its scheduled departure. After the parade, Wiley and Gatty posed with Mayor Walker on the steps of City Hall, while flash bulbs popped incessantly. The fliers were presented with solid gold medals to commemorate their flight. The mayor quipped that the *Winnie Mae* must have been the Winnie Must while flying over Siberia and the Winnie Did when they arrived at Roosevelt Field, "the victors over time and space."

A newspaper story under the headline "TRIBUTE AT CITY HALL AMAZES MODEST PAIR" described the tumultuous reception:

> The Mayor greeted them with characteristic quips and jests, while the fliers stood stiffly on the flag-draped platform. The harsh light of studio lamps glared in their eyes and their feet were enmeshed in a tangle of microphone wires and sound-reel paraphernalia. Nearly 400 persons had jammed themselves into the room, which was stuffy and warm.[162]

Dr. John H. Finley, chairman of the mayor's committee for the reception of distinguished guests, lauded Wiley and Gatty, "They have carried a new strand of human kinship around the globe, a globe which is smaller today than ever it has been before in the history of its ages."

Wiley thanked Mayor Walker and the whole city of New York for its rousing welcome and celebration. He spoke bashfully, with his hands in his pockets, and later admitted that it was his first public speech. A friend observed, "All Wiley knows how to do is to fly. He doesn't know how to talk. A flier like Wiley can't be bothered to talk."

Wiley spoke seriously about the impact of their flight in a special story written for the *New York Times* July 3 edition:

> We think we really have accomplished something more than tearing around the world faster than anybody ever made it before. We have great hopes that we may have helped bring the time closer when commercial aviation will span the seas and the land, and bring all peoples closer together...
>
> One thing I learned is that a man can sit in a plane, stay there for hours, be perfectly safe and get where he is going to even if he can't see anything beyond the instrument board. We did that repeatedly in this flight, and I would think that the general public's just knowing that such a thing was possible would increase confidence in aviation.[163]

While Wiley and Gatty and their wives were being treated as heroes, the *Winnie Mae* was flown from Roosevelt Field to Floyd Bennett Field. Thousands paraded by the airplane during the weekend it was on display.

President Herbert Hoover invited Wiley and Gatty and their wives to the White House in Washington, D. C. Flanked by members of his cabinet, Hoover congratulated Wiley and Gatty on their "courage, determination, technical ability, and skill." During lunch, the President and Gatty found out they shared a great love, fishing. Wiley later chided Gatty for monopolizing the conversation, "This guy (Gatty) is an old fisherman and he stole the whole show. I didn't know anything about 32-thread line, but he sure did."

Before returning to New York, Wiley and Gatty appeared before the National Press Club. Several thousand people watched the club's president Eugene S. Leggett present the fliers with medals. Then Wiley and Gatty and their larger-than-life escorts went to a movie theater where they saw motion pictures of the beginning and ending of their flight.

Back in New York, The Aeronautical Chamber of Commerce hosted a dinner at the famed Astor Hotel. Five hundred people attended the banquet that featured a presentation of special plaques to Wiley and Gatty recognizing their achievement.

Wherever Wiley went, his fans wanted to know how he stayed awake while at the controls of the *Winnie Mae*. He had slept a total of only 15 hours in eight and half days, but his answer was simple, "I didn't get sleepy. I was tired, but I had little problem staying awake." He explained that the secret of his success lay in being focused and relaxed completely while he was in the pilot's seat. The *New York Times*, in an editorial entitled, "A Feat of Endurance," opined that Wiley's skill and daring was overshadowed by his ability to undergo prolonged physical strain and the flight was "proof of what men could endure when necessary."[164]

Wiley and Gatty slept only a few hours the first two days they were back on the ground. A newspaper reporter interviewed them at the Ritz-Carlton Hotel as they sat "side by side on a divan" near a window facing the numerous reporters who were seated on chairs, beds, a table, a dresser and a radiator. Wiley, "coatless, wearing a blue shirt with a trim bow tie," had a tired expression about his eyes and yawned frequently. He failed to respond to several questions. Gatty relayed one to him. "I can hear a bit," said Wiley, "I'll be able to hear all right in a day or two. I can hear better in a ship than on the ground. I miss the noise here."[165]

The American aviation community marveled at the technical success of the *Winnie Mae*. Other than when Wiley changed out four sparkplugs in Russia, the airplane required minimal servicing. The Wasp engine never sputtered even though strange gasoline in strange places ran through her lines.

BACK HOME IN OKLAHOMA

He's a determined looking little rascal—
WILL ROGERS

OKLAHOMANS were especially proud of Wiley for his history-making flight. The *Maysville News* said, "Maysville has been placed on the map of the world along with such places as New York, Berlin, Blagoveshchensk, Khabarovsk and Irkutsk."[166]

Thousands of admiring fans saluted Wiley and Gatty as they walked behind a motorcycle escort in a parade through downtown Oklahoma City, July 10, 1931. Courtesy *The Daily Oklahoman.*

Wiley's hometown paper equated his feats with those of Columbus, Magellan, and Lindbergh and correctly stated that Wiley "would rather fly around the world than make a five minute speech."

Across America, magazines and newspapers printed every angle of the Post-Gatty flight. The nation was in the grips of the Great Depression and the real-life adventure story was the talk of the day. It gave Americans hope and something to believe in.

Wiley's aviation exploits made celebrities out of F.C. Hall, (left) Winnie Mae Hall Fain, (right), and her husband, Leslie Fain. Courtesy *The Daily Oklahoman.*

Oklahoma Governor William H. "Alfalfa Bill" Murray welcomed Wiley and Gatty after they landed the *Winnie Mae* at Chickasha July 10, 1931. F.C. Hall had made a deal with a Chickasha newspaper that the first stop in Oklahoma after the successful completion of the trip would be in Chickasha. (L to R) F.C. Hall, Wiley, Governor Murray, Gatty. Courtesy Oklahoma Historical Society.

F. C. Hall made a deal with the *Chickasha Daily Express* for Wiley's first public appearance back in Oklahoma to be in Chickasha. Wiley, Gatty, and Hall arrived in Chickasha in the *Winnie Mae* on July 9, a day described by the Chickasha mayor as "the biggest event in Oklahoma since the opening of the Cherokee Strip."[167] Oklahoma Governor William H. "Alfalfa Bill" Murray and U.S. Senator Thomas Gore led the official delegation that met the plane and the returning heroes.

Wiley's sister Mary was the first member of the family to greet Wiley. They embraced without speaking and both smiled broadly. While Wiley and Gatty were posing for pictures, Wiley's parents were driven to the field. His mother said, "Wiley, bless your heart, you blessed thing," while kissing him and patting him on the shoulder. Mr. Post walked up and shook hands with his son and, without a word, turned and shook hands with Gatty.

A young father was so overwhelmed with the sight of the *Winnie Mae* that he named his new baby girl after the airplane. J. G. McClain of Oklahoma City later wrote Gatty that he let his newborn touch the plane and christened her "*Winnie Mae*" McClain.

Oklahoma City held a banquet the next day in honor of Wiley and Gatty. It was broadcast nationally on CBS radio.

Native Oklahoman Will Rogers was without question the most popular American of his day. He was a vaudeville and film star,

Wiley gave Will Rogers his first ride in the *Winnie Mae* at Claremore a few days after Wiley and Gatty completed their 1931 trip around the world. Will (in the straw hat) is flanked by Wiley and Gatty and local officials. Will, never at a loss for words, told a banquet audience about Wiley, "He is a determined looking little rascal, and when he says quit, you can bet there would be no more gas, or no more air." Courtesy *The Daily Oklahoman.*

champion roper, radio commentator, and the most widely read newspaper columnist in the world. He was best known as a humorist, but one whose opinions received serious attention. He could probably have been elected President, but wanted no part of politics, he just wanted to joke about the politicians.

Will was an early supporter of aviation's role in the future of America, calling it the greatest advancement in his time. His newspaper columns often mentioned the adventures of aviation pioneers. If any flight record was broken, Will wrote about it. When radar for airplanes was invented, Will was on top of the story.

When Wiley and Gatty completed their globe-circling trip in eight days, Will told the nation: "No news today as big as this Post and Gatty that are making this world of ours like the size of a watermelon."[168]

Will had never met Wiley until after the 1931 around-the-world flight when Will's nephew, Bruce Quisenberry, took Wiley and Gatty to Will's home in Santa Monica, California. Quisenberry managed a Post-Gatty nationwide speaking tour sponsored by the Mobil Oil Company. Wiley and Will hit it off immediately and talked into the wee hours about airplanes and flying.

Will wrote a column patting F. C. Hall on the back for bankrolling Wiley's record-breaking flight. When Hall responded informing Will that his hometown of Claremore was throwing a reception for the fliers, Will wrote that Wiley probably would not go to Claremore because it had no airport. Within five days, city and chamber of commerce officials built an airport in Claremore.

Will decided to attend the Claremore banquet for Wiley and Gatty. He arrived late but was asked to speak. As usual, Will Rogers had plenty to say. His marvelous introduction of Wiley appears as the Introduction to this book.

Will called the wives of Wiley and Gatty the real heroes:

Here they sit enjoying a fleeing bit of adulation. But who were the real heroes of this trip? Didn't their bravery in letting the boys go make it possible? What do you think they did through those eight days? How much did they sleep? The person doing the thing gets the constant thrill, but the one waiting only gets the grief. So it took more than Mr. Hall with his generosity, Mr. Post with his skill, Mr. Gatty with his knowledge, and Mr. Somebody with his round world to bring this about. Behind it all, it took the sacrifice and courage of two women. So let's give a toast to Mrs. Gatty and Mrs. Post and the wives of every flier, for they are the heroes.[169]

Will could not have known how much the flight had strained relations between Harold Gatty and his wife, who were divorced a few months later.

After the banquet at Claremore, Wiley gave Will his first ride in the *Winnie Mae*. He wrote in his July 14 column:

It's the combination of the two (Post and Gatty) that makes 'em so great. I'd bet on 'em going around the world endways and cross both poles. In all the excitement and rushing about, you know when they sleep? At the banquets. They said if it wasn't for banquets they wouldn't have any time to sleep at all.

Will's friendship with Wiley grew stronger. At every opportunity Will mentioned Wiley's black eye patch, Will called it "a mark of distinction."

The flight of Wiley and Gatty inspired newspaper reporters with new and inventive terms for aviation. The *Winnie Mae* was called a "lady-plane from Oklahoma that put a girdle around the earth." The Birmingham, Alabama *News* said the airplane should be "commissioned to race with the sun and the moon and the stars."

IS THAT ALL THERE IS?

If there is a hell upon earth, it is to be found in a melancholy
man's heart—

ROBERT BURTON,

THE ANATOMY OF MELANCHOLY, 1 8 4 5

N THE 1 9 6 0 S, singer Peggy Lee released a hit song entitled "Is That All There Is?" The lyrics of the song detail her
rich accomplishments in life, but she is always left with the
question, "Is that all there is?" Wiley had similar feelings after his
around-the-world flight in 1931. Even though the whole world
considered him a hero, he thought of himself as an under-achiever
and openly said he had done nothing to further the cause of aviation.

As America continued to honor Wiley and Gatty, other fliers
began to make plans to best the new record for an around-the-
world flight. Within a few days of the end of the Post-Gatty flight,
Hugh Herndon and Clyde Pangborn told reporters that their Bellanca airplane could beat the *Winnie Mae's* record. They admitted
the Bellanca was slower than the Lockheed Vega flown by Wiley,
but the greater range of their plane would eliminate ten of the
thirteen stops made by Wiley and Gatty. Other fliers convinced
their backers that Wiley and Gatty had opened up aviation for the
whole world, resulting in a flood of record-breaking attempts over
the next two years.

The goodwill tour, in a different city every day, grew tiring.
Wiley and Hall had strong differences on how much Wiley could
use the *Winnie Mae* in personal appearances around the country.

The *Oklahoma City Times* adequately explained the plight of the world heroes, "Almost broke, their plans for the future a little indefinite, a couple of young men who were in a hurry around the world a few months ago, slowed down considerably Monday and took an accounting of their adventures. Post reportedly said that he would clear about $500 for his part of the flight."[170]

Hall had agreed shortly after the completion of the flight to sell the *Winnie Mae* to Wiley for $21,200, $3,000 down within 30 days and a note for $18,200. The sales contract provided that the name of the plane would be changed if *Winnie Mae* Fain desired. Fortunately, Mrs. Fain had no problem with her name being splashed around the world. She "was content to permit Wiley Post and his Vega to carry her name on into history."[171]

After the *Winnie Mae* was sold to Wiley, Hall purchased a new Lockheed Vega and named it *Winnie Mae* of Oklahoma City, Okla. Hall bragged to reporters that his new plane could break Wiley and Gatty's record. But Hall never tried it, sold the plane a year later, and faded into aviation history.

Less than a month after arriving at Roosevelt Field, Wiley announced the possibility that he would attempt a non-stop flight from Tokyo to Seattle. No one yet had flown across the Pacific. Wiley proposed several changes in the *Winnie Mae*, including a landing gear that could be jettisoned. Two months later, Herndon and Pangborn made a successful trans-Pacific flight from Japan to Wenatchee, Washington. Wiley only liked to do challenging things, so he called off his flight from Tokyo. Mohler and Johnson said, "Wiley Post always tried to do new things, and in new ways, that would leave a historic milestone along the path of progress of manned flight. He was not a man who poured old wine into new bottles; it was not his way to fly in the tracks of other men, simply for the sake of setting a new record."[172]

In August, Rand McNally and Company hired writer Leo Kieran to work with Wiley and Gatty on a book about their flying adventure. *Around the World in Eight Days,* printed on cheap paper in just three weeks, never received the attention and respect it deserved.

When he wasn't in "the wild blue yonder," Wiley liked to take his best shotgun and go hunting with his friends. This 1932 hunting trip was near Tishimingo in southern Oklahoma. (L to R) George Van Noy, Ray White, Wiley, Ted Colbert. Courtesy Oklahoma Historical Society.

Wiley was exhausted and took off September and October to hunt ducks and quail in Texas and old Mexico. In November he appeared in Chicago obviously disenchanted with his future in aviation. In an interview with a newspaper reporter, Wiley said he felt his trip around the world had done nothing for aviation and that the economics made it almost impossible for him to earn any money in flying. The reporter described Wiley as "a little hard of hearing, plump, genial and disillusioned."[173]

The hearing problem was easily explained. Wiley had temporarily lost part of his hearing because of the long hours of exposure to the noisy Wasp engine on the *Winnie Mae*. The "plump" description also could be explained. Wiley had actually lost weight during the eight days around the world, but had picked up 20 pounds during the wining and dining around the nation in the months after the flight. The "disillusioned" tag worried Mae and Wiley's friends.

The outside world only saw a victorious, famous flier who had conquered the air in his jaunt around the earth. Not even Mae was fully aware of the "melancholy" problem that Wiley had suffered during his 13 months in prison a decade before.

"Melancholy" is an obsolete diagnostic term that today refers to "pronounced depression with feelings of foreboding, cognitive changes, and a general insensitivity to stimulation."[174] Depression has been part of the human condition for thousands of years and has been described in many ways, from "demonic possession" to "biochemical disturbance."

One of the more popular early explanations of the malady of melancholy was a surplus of *melan chole,* the Greek term for black bile.

Oklahoma City psychologist Stephen Carella has written that Wiley Post, with his diagnosis of melancholy, joined a long list of outstanding individuals such as Edgar Allan Poe, Nathaniel Hawthorne, Abraham Lincoln, Winston Churchill, Charles Darwin, and astronaut Edwin "Buzz" Aldrin Jr., all of whom endured serious problems with depression.

Wiley poses with his car at Northeast 18th and Lincoln Boulevard in Oklahoma City in 1932. The State Capitol building is in the background. To its right is the Oklahoma Historical Society Building, later named for Wiley. Courtesy Oklahoma Historical Society.

George Washington suffered from numerous psychosomatic ills that appear to be depression-linked. Abraham Lincoln, as a young man, was so withdrawn and brooding that his friends feared he might take his own life. Churchill called his periods of depression his "black dog of depression." When Charles Darwin returned from his fossil collecting voyage, "he had to lay the work aside for a year and a half because he became so depressed that he could not even read."[175]

Wiley's state of depression after flying the *Winnie Mae* around the earth in 1931 was similar to the depression that plagued Buzz Aldrin, the second man to walk on the moon. Dr. Carella compared the two aviators and their depression problems:

> Buzz Aldrin stated that he was on his way to having "a good old American nervous breakdown." He was hospitalized for approximately a month and received help for his melancholy. So as you can see, with the 1922 diagnosis of melancholy, Wiley Post joined the ranks of very distinguished scholars, scientists, and astronauts who altered the world. In fact, these very achievements may have actually contributed to their depressions.[176]

For the remainder of his short life, Wiley's moods ranged from extremely happy to gloomy and sad. He often wanted to be completely alone, the "perfect" psychological trait necessary for a human being to fly around the world. . . alone.

Wiley looked for some way, any way, to fund another trip around the world. Economic woes caused by the Great Depression had dried up extra money that the rich might use to fund daring pilots in their attempts to break aviation records. The Smithsonian Institution in Washington offered to buy the *Winnie Mae* if Wiley could launch a drive to raise contributions for the purchase.

Wiley shelved the notion of selling his plane, because the idea of another flight around the world began to occupy his every waking moment. The *Winnie Mae* was not ready for a museum. . . not yet.

Part
Three

ANOTHER DREAM

She's one of the finest outfitted planes in the world—

T O M   B R A N I F F

MOST OF 1932 was lost time for Wiley. His pilot's log reflected less than 20 hours of flying between March and September. The nation's newspapers were void of any mention of the famous pilot who still dreamed of soloing around the world in his *Winnie Mae.*

The first clue as to Wiley's intentions show up in government records surrounding the transfer of ownership of the *Winnie Mae.* Early in 1933, the "Fain and Post Drilling Company" bought the plane from *Winnie Mae* Fain. Apparently Wiley had sold the aircraft to her because he could not make the promised payments to her father. Wiley applied for a restricted license for the aircraft to make a solo around-the-world flight. Leslie Fain, Winnie Mae Fain's husband, was listed as the president of the company and Wiley was listed as the secretary-treasurer. No one knew anything about the drilling company and Wiley refused to answer reporters' questions about his plans.

The February 19, 1933 edition of the *New York Times* predicted that Wiley would soon make another trip around the world. Again, Wiley refused to comment. The newspaper story, quoting reliable sources, indicated Wiley would fly alone and would use a new "robot" or automatic pilot.

Wiley was in a tight race with Jimmy Mattern to see who could solo around the world first. Mattern had teamed up with Bennett Griffin in July, 1932, to attempt to best the eight-day around-the-world record of Wiley and Gatty. Mattern and Griffin specially equipped a Lockheed Vega named *Century of Progress* with the cabin fuel tanks used in the *Winnie Mae* in the 1931 flight. Wiley had sold the tanks in hopes that he could come up with even better ideas to make the *Winnie Mae* more efficient in future flights.

On July 5, 1932, almost exactly a year after Wiley and Gatty's flight, Mattern and Griffin took off for Harbor Grace and successfully reached Berlin. However, they were forced to crash land in Russia when the cabin hatch flew off and damaged the plane in flight. The wings and fuselage were so heavily damaged in the crash that the fliers had to bring the plane back to America in pieces.[177]

Wiley received encouragement for his 1933 solo flight around the world from aviation hero Charles Lindbergh. (L to R), Wiley, Lindbergh, and Bennett Griffin, a skilled pilot who also had visions of being the first person to solo around the earth. Courtesy Oklahoma Historical Society.

When Mattern and Griffin learned Wiley was planning a solo trip around the earth, they flipped a coin to see who would try to beat him. Mattern won, purchased a new Vega from the Standard Oil Company of New Jersey, and began planning.

Wiley would have preferred an updated aircraft for his attempt. The *Winnie Mae*, made by Lockheed primarily out of plywood, was becoming obsolete. New twin-engine, all-metal aircraft were being manufactured and tested. However, a new airplane was far beyond Wiley's financial capability, so he began the process of preparing the *Winnie Mae* for the flight.

In March, 1933, Wiley was authorized by the Department of Commerce Aeronautics Branch to install a Sperry automatic pilot to assist him in flying alone around the globe. The Sperry version of the automatic pilot, which Wiley called "Mechanical Mike," was the most sophisticated and reliable of its kind in the early 1930s.

It differed from previous autopilots in an important manner. Other automatic pilots of the time used electrical "pick offs" to determine the relative motions of the aircraft and the "fixed" axes of the spinning gyroscopes, and utilized a slip-stream "wind-powered" spinning gear device as the motive power to enable the autopilot to move the control surfaces. Wiley's pilot used airjet pickoffs and was completely mechanical and did not use electrical power. The entire apparatus weighed 70 pounds and had not been fully tested when Wiley installed it in his plane.[178]

The federal government gave Wiley permission to install the autopilot in his plane on the condition that he not carry any passengers for hire. To a knowledgeable observer, that meant only one thing, that Wiley was planning something special and he would be flying alone, with only a "robot" or autopilot as his companion.

Wiley tested the new autopilot in late March on a trip from Oklahoma City to Mexico. The system worked efficiently and allowed Wiley to fly long distances without constantly manning the controls.

Carelessness almost cost Wiley his life on April 21 at an airport south of Chickasha. Wiley wanted veteran pilot Luther E. "Red"

Wiley and Amelia Earhart (right) greatly respected each other's ability as pilots. Earhart gave Wiley much of the credit for her success on long-distance flights in the early 1930's. Courtesy Oklahoma Historical Society.

Gray to fly the *Winnie Mae* to test the autopilot. Gray was joined in the aircraft by Wiley, young Oklahoma City businessman, Harry G. Frederickson, and another passenger. Gray noticed that the fuel gauge indicated "empty," but Wiley persuaded Gray to take off because he had recently refueled the plane and thought surely there was enough gas for a short test flight. What Wiley did not know was that teenagers had slipped into the airport under cover of darkness and siphoned all of the plane's gas for their cars.

Gray gunned the engine and headed down the turf runway. When the plane reached an altitude of about 50 feet, the engine suddenly quit. Gray hoped to bring the *Winnie Mae* back to earth, and ground-looped before running into a peach orchard at the end of the field. Gray's experience in flying Vegas for Braniff Airways apparently saved the *Winnie Mae* from complete destruction when she finally did strike the trees.[179]

The plane's occupants were lucky. Wiley had only a cut finger, Frederickson suffered two cracked ribs, and Gray and the other passenger were unhurt.

The *Winnie Mae* was badly shaken up in the crash in Chickasha so Wiley hauled her to the Braniff Airways repair shop at Curtis-Wright Field in Oklahoma City. Braniff was a major player in the early aviation picture, especially in the central section of the United States. Paul Braniff had begun flying passengers between Oklahoma City and Tulsa in 1928, an air service that would later become Braniff International.

"Red" Gray was a pilot for Braniff, so the company wanted to do what it could to repair the *Winnie Mae*. A master German woodworker, George Brauer, supervised the body work on the plywood fuselage of the airplane.

When the repairs were completed, Wiley could not come up with but $1,200.00 of the $1,763.92 necessary to reimburse Braniff. Five Braniff employees, pilots "Red" Gray and Claude Seaton, head mechanic Sterling E. Perry, Brauer, and operations manager Tom Braniff donated their time so Wiley could resume his preparations for his dream trip. Wiley later made sure that they were paid double for their donated hours.[180]

Brauer designed and placed large fuel tanks in the *Winnie Mae*'s cabin, raising the plane's fuel capacity to 645 gallons. Other critical changes were made. A radio mast made of one-inch diameter streamlined tubing, six feet long, was installed in the fin and a new Breeze radio-shielded ignition harness was put on the engine.[181]

Pratt and Whitney sent their crack mechanic Raymond Peck to Oklahoma City to supervise modifications to the Wasp engine. New cylinder heads and sodium-cooled exhaust valves were used. State-of-the-art rocker boxes were added that allowed Wiley to use a grease gun to grease the rocker arms during flight. That unique innovation reduced the likelihood of in-flight emergencies and cut down on ground maintenance.

When the Braniff employees rolled the *Winnie Mae* out of their shop in early May, she was "one of the finest outfitted airplanes in the world." On May 19, Assistant Secretary of Commerce Clarence M. Young made the first public announcement of Wiley's proposed flight when he asked the U. S. State Department to request permission for Wiley to land in Newfoundland, Ireland, Great Britain, Belgium, and Poland. Young wrote that the Commerce Department did not object to the flight, approved the plane as airworthy, and the pilot as competent. The letter listed the owner of the *Winnie Mae* as "Winnie Mae Fain, 624 Culbertson Drive, Oklahoma City, Oklahoma."[182]

Finally, in May, Wiley announced details of his planned flight in an interview with *New York Times* aviation editor Lauren Lyman. The story appeared in the May 28, 1933 edition of the paper and predicted that Wiley would fly nonstop from New York to Berlin, almost 4,000 miles. That was 1,000 miles farther than the Vega could normally fly without refueling, but Wiley told the *Times* he could fly up to 4,000 miles because of the modifications made in his plane, specifically extra fuel tanks and the addition of a Smith controllable-pitch prop.[183]

The Smith propeller was entirely mechanical in operation. It required no hydraulic or electrical system, and was quickly recognized by the three-sixteenths-inch hole drilled near the tip of each blade. The holes drained water out of the hollow blades.[184]

Wiley planned only five refueling stops: Berlin, Novosibirsk, Kharbarovsk, Fairbanks, and Edmonton, compared with 14 stops on the 1931 flight.

Wiley was a guest of honor for the May 15 dedication of a new Oklahoma City Municipal Airport. For years the city's main airport had been located at Southwest 29th and May. Aviation pioneer Clarence Page and the Oklahoma City Chamber of Commerce pushed through a bond issue in 1929 that made possible the purchase of 640 acres near Portland and Southwest 59th for the new Municipal Airport, later called Will Rogers Field and now Will Rogers World Airport.[185]

Wiley still needed someone to bankroll his "date" with history.

F. C. Hall's purse was no longer "at hand to be tapped," and by 1933 the Great Depression was at rock bottom and the resources of the wealthy oilmen who assisted in financing the 1931 flight were no longer available.[186]

Into the picture came Harry G. Frederickson, who had his ribs cracked in the Chickasha crash. Frederickson made a deal with Wiley to raise money for the flight for a ten percent commission. Wiley's only requirement was that contributions should come only from Oklahomans who were truly interested in aviation.

Frederickson's first stop was the Oklahoma City Chamber of Commerce and its director, Stanley Draper, a driving force in making Oklahoma a center of early aviation activity. Draper appointed a committee to help Frederickson and made the first contribution.

The Chamber of Commerce sponsored a citywide luncheon to solicit funds. However, it was not until *Daily Oklahoman* editor Walter M. Harrison picked up the torch for the flight that citizens began to enthusiastically endorse Wiley and put their pocketbooks where their mouths were.

Forty-one individuals and businesses contributed the $40,000 Wiley needed. The list read like a *Who's Who* of Oklahoma history: Newspaper reporter A. S. "Mike" Monroney, who later served as U. S. Representative and U. S. Senator and led America's aviation efforts in Congress for decades; Yukon miller John Kroutill; oilman Frank Phillips; former Oklahoma Governor Lee Cruce; Tom Braniff; Congressman Gomer Smith; the Oklahoma Publishing Company (publisher of *The Daily Oklahoman*); Stanley Draper; W. E. Hightower; Virgil Browne, who became one of the nation's leading soft-drink bottling executives; Oklahoma Natural Gas Company; attorney O. A. Cargill; John A. Brown; S. F. Veazey, known for his famous drug store; W. E. Grisso; and L. A. Macklanburg.

Wiley persuaded many of the country's leading aircraft manufacturers and suppliers to donate supplies and equipment. Pratt and Whitney donated the time of a technical specialist, Lionel B. Clark; the Sperry Gyroscope Company donated the autopilot; and

Mobil Oil provided the fuel, oil, and grease necessary to make the trip. Even the Roosevelt Hotel in New York got into the spirit of giving by providing a $35-a-day suite for Wiley's use before and after the flight.

The U. S. Army Signal Corps installed a new radio direction finder in the *Winnie Mae*. Radio beams assisted pilots to stay on a predetermined course, regardless of wind and visibility conditions. The system allowed pilots to be entirely independent of any ground system and was referred to as the automatic direction finder (ADF). It involved a fixed "loop" antenna which was attached to the outside of the plane. Few details of the ADF were released to the press because the military was still testing the device. It later would become standard equipment on all American military aircraft.

Newspapers were told, "By tuning to a standard broadcast station, Post could determine the bearing from his position to the station, and turn so as to fly toward (or away from) the station." A popular flying magazine, the *Scientific American,* reported that Wiley would use radio stations at St. John's, Newfoundland, Manchester, England, and other private and government radio stations in Russia and Alaska.

Wiley used the same training methods to prepare for his new dream that he had utilized before the 1931 flight. He limited his intake of food and broke his regular sleeping habits. He often spent all night at the airport, sitting alone in the cockpit of the *Winnie Mae* with his eye open.[187]

On June 1, Wiley began a series of test flights in final preparation for his flight around the world. Time was short because Wiley had just received word that Jimmy Mattern and his airplane were ready to go.

MATTERN LIFTS OFF FIRST

See you in six days or else—

W I L E Y   P O S T

WILEY'S HOPE of being the first person to fly solo around the earth was dashed when he heard a radio broadcast on June 3, 1933, reporting that Jimmy Mattern had begun his flight around the world. A friendly rivalry had developed between Wiley and Mattern, now direct competitors for one of the great honors in history. Wiley told the press that he would not be rushed, he would begin his flight when his aircraft was ready, and the weather ideal, and not a minute sooner.

Mattern took off from Floyd Bennett Field in New York in his Vega *Century of Progress.* The world's newspapers began to cover the flight in depth. Wiley was not shaken by Mattern's attempt and said even if Mattern made it around the world in four days, he, Wiley, would not attempt the solo flight until every detail of his elaborate plan was ready.

Mattern made it to Norway in just under 24 hours, refueled, and headed eastward to Moscow. Ten days later, Mattern took off from Kharbarovsk in Siberia for Nome, Alaska, but never made it.

For two weeks the world wondered in horror about Mattern's fate. It was July 5 before news came that Mattern was alive. Somehow he had survived to tell the story of his engine simply stopping over the wilds of the Siberian tundra. He made an emergency crash landing near the Anadyr River, built a raft, and floated to civilization where he was rescued by a band of Eskimos.

Meanwhile, Wiley went about his business of preparing the *Winnie Mae* for the flight. On June 10, Braniff Airways maintenance superintendent S. E. Perry signed a Department of Commerce Certificate of Repairs on the plane. Two dozen changes were noted. The entire fuselage was covered with balloon cloth, the cockpit had been completely rebuilt, all new control cables were installed, wing and fuselage fuel tanks with a total capacity of 645 gallons were installed, the entire landing gear was rebuilt, all bolts and nuts replaced, the Wasp 450-horsepower engine was overhauled and new magnetos and a new Breeze radio-shielding ignition harness were installed. The *Winnie Mae* was ready to take on the world.[188]

Wiley and Harry Frederickson flew from Oklahoma City to New York's Floyd Bennett Field on June 14. Bennett Field, located on Long Island's Jamaica Bay, was New York City's first municipal airport, and was named after a great American aviator who was Richard Byrd's pilot on their flight to the North Pole in 1926. The airport is now known as John F. Kennedy International Airport.

An unusual problem surrounded the *Winnie Mae* for the next few days. Someone tried to damage the engine and the carburetor, and Wiley received threatening letters. Wiley hired security guards to watch over him and his airplane. Since the top-secret ADF had been installed in the plane, the U.S. Army also placed guards around the *Winnie Mae*.

Wiley had become famous, and fame often draws weird people out of their caves. *The Daily Oklahoman*, on June 27, reported that an inventor wanted a sample of Wiley's blood to test a machine he had developed, a machine that would keep contact between Wiley's blood in a bottle and Wiley himself anywhere in the world. Wiley reacted by hiring more security guards.

As in 1931, Wiley again had to wait out the North Atlantic weather before beginning his around-the-world flight in 1933. Dr. James Kimball of the U.S. Weather Bureau was once more Wiley's premier weather adviser. Squalls and cold fronts over the ocean kept Wiley grounded for four weeks. Every time the weather appeared to breaking up, along came another storm. Friends and

Wiley had lots of support for his 1933 solo attempt. (L to R) Lee Trenholm
(Wiley's business manager), Wiley, Bennie Turner (who had been sent by *The Daily
Oklahoman* to New York to cover the flight), and Harry G. Frederickson, the
Oklahoma City oil man who raised the money necessary to fund the trip. This
photo was taken at Floyd Bennett Field in New York, July 5, 1933. Courtesy
Oklahoma Historical Society.

fans of Wiley came to the airport each time it was announced that
the flight would begin, only to be disappointed by another delay.
Finally, on Saturday, July 15, Dr. Kimball's forecast was promising,
and Wiley decided it was time to go.

Because of the many false starts, only 500 people were on hand for Wiley's big moment. When Wiley appeared on the field he was dressed in a "snappy new dark gray double-breasted suit, which was worn over a white shirt with a blue necktie." Wiley refused to wear the customary flying clothes and to "look like an aviator." Many fliers in the late 1920s and early 1930s wore cavalry boots and carefully tailored riding breeches with fancy leather jackets, and helmets and goggles. They looked like someone out of the "Smilin' Jack" or "Tailspin Tommy" comic strips. But not Wiley Post. The only thing that prevented Wiley from looking like a New York businessman en route to the office was his lack of a hat.[189]

Wiley wore a white patch over his left eye, a change from the 1931 flight. Then, Wiley had used his glass eye, which became so cold over Siberia and Alaska, it gave him a severe headache.

The *New York Times* detailed the equipment and personal belongings Wiley would take with him on the flight. He planned to carry an overnight bag with clean linen and other necessities, including three fresh eye patches for his sightless eye. As emergency equipment he planned to take quart thermos bottles of water and tomato juice, three packages of chewing gum, a package of zwieback [German sweet bread], a knife, a hatchet, a raincoat, fishing tackle, a cigarette lighter, a pocket transit, mosquito netting, a sleeping bag and a pocket searchlight.[190]

Gathered around the *Winnie Mae* were Wiley's closest supporters. Mae, Harry Frederickson, Lee Trenholm (Wiley's business manager), and Bennie Turner, a reporter for *The Daily Oklahoman* stood close by. Wiley borrowed a pencil and paper and sent a telegram to *Oklahoman* editor Walter Harrison, extending his thanks to all the people who were making the flight possible.

Wiley turned to Mae, kissed her good-bye, and said, "See you in six days or else." Wiley jumped up on the *Winnie Mae* and dropped through the open hatch into the cockpit. One of the great moments in the history of humankind was about to begin.

THE EPIC FLIGHT

His face was drawn and his one good eye bloodshot—

OTTO TOLISCHUS, *NEW YORK TIMES*

AS A HINT of daybreak began to "spread itself across the low marshes and swampland," the *Winnie Mae* stood poised at the Flatbush Avenue end of the Floyd Bennett runway that pointed toward Jamaica Bay. She was fueled "to her caps" with 645 gallons of gasoline. At 5:10 A.M., July 15, 1933, Wiley checked the 14-degree pitch setting of his propeller, ran his eye over the instrument panel, and opened his throttle. He released the brakes and the *Winnie Mae* went charging down the runway. Her tail came up, and after a 1,900 foot run of only 29 seconds, the "hard-working rubber of her tires left the runway." She was airborne—and on her way around the world, again.[191]

Wiley lifted off with ease from Floyd Bennett Field, a takeoff described by a reporter as one that "sent tingles up the spines of even the hardened onlookers." The small, white airplane grew smaller as reporters, friends, and well-wishers were left behind on the runway. Mae followed Wiley for the first few miles with pilot "Red" Gray in a white Lockheed Vega similar to the *Winnie Mae*. Mae described the historical moment, "Red took me up and we flew along beside him until he disappeared into the fog. For a little while, I didn't know if he would make it off the runway because the plane was loaded with so much gasoline. That plane really trembled from the load, but he made it."[192]

The Sperry autopilot was given its first test only five minutes into the flight. Wiley ran into thick fog and turned the autopilot on. It worked perfectly. For most of the next two hours, Wiley flew blindly with the use of his new "Mechanical Mike."

After he passed the rocky shores of Nova Scotia, Wiley tuned his radio to a station at St. John's, Newfoundland, a station predetermined to assist him in using his radio compass. He also received valuable, updated weather information from the St. John's station.

The skies over the North Atlantic were kinder to Wiley on this trip than they had been in 1931. He was able to fly at 2,000 feet in clear skies halfway across the Atlantic. Then he ran into the front that had kept him grounded in New York for days. He climbed to 11,000 feet, only to find more rain and clouds.

Will Rogers closely followed Wiley's solo flight. In his July 16 news column, Rogers said, "I will bet you that this Wiley Post makes it around the world and breaks his own record, I would have liked to have been in there with Post instead of the robot."

Aviation had advanced lightyears since 1931. Wiley's flight with Gatty had been lonely with hardly any radio contact. This time Wiley picked up radio station G2LO in Manchester, England, and heard a special broadcast that started with the words, "This is a special broadcast for Wiley Post." Wiley tuned his radio compass and began flying toward jolly old England. As Wiley flew closer to the European continent, his ADF was able to receive even more radio stations, a great help to his navigation.

Wiley flew above the clouds over Ireland but dropped under an overcast sky to cross the Irish Sea to Great Britain and eastward to Germany. In just under 26 hours from takeoff in New York he landed in Berlin. It was not quite 7:00 A.M. on Sunday, July 16, when history's first non-stop flight from New York to Berlin ended. The *Winnie Mae* had flown the 3,942 miles at an average of 153.5 miles per hour, shattering the previous trans-Atlantic records of Lindbergh and Clarence Chamberlin. Both had averaged only about 100 miles per hour with the 200-horsepower engines of the *Spirit of St. Louis* and the *Liberty,* compared to the 500-plus-horsepower *Winnie Mae.*

Wiley was numb and virtually deaf when he hopped out of his plane in Berlin. When a high-ranking German colonel congratulated him upon his arrival, all he could do was nod, shake the colonel's hand and say, "Let's get her gassed up again." A squad of

German soldiers, replete with swastika armbands, kept the crowd at bay as airport crews began refueling the *Winnie Mae.* Wiley calculated his airplane's performance on the almost 4,000-mile hike through the skies of the North Atlantic. He had used only 485 gallons of fuel, an economical 19 gallons per hour. The *Winnie Mae* still contained 160 gallons of gasoline.

It was a far different Germany in 1933 than when Wiley had landed there in 1931. In January, 1933, German president Field Marshall von Hindenburg had appointed Nazi party leader Adolph Hitler as chancellor. Hitler promised the Germans they would be rich and dominant again. Inflation and high unemployment had plagued the country since its defeat in World War I. Hitler flattered the Germans into thinking they were a master race. He would become president and dictator of Germany when von Hindenburg died in 1934.

A large crowd greeted Wiley in Berlin, among them Herman Goering, German World War I ace, who recently had been appointed by Adolph Hitler as the Chief of the German Air Ministry.[193]

New York Times correspondent Otto Tolischus described Wiley's physical condition, "Post plainly showed the effects of his flight across the ocean. His dark gray suit was spic and span, but his face was drawn and his one good eye was bloodshot."[194]

Officials insisted that Wiley see a local doctor, Colonel Wuest. Wiley assured the Colonel he was all right and laid down on a couch to rest. Twenty minutes later he was back at the side of his airplane and took charge of the refueling. Wiley again sold the exclusive rights to his personal account of the trip to the *New York Times.* When he arrived in Berlin, he cabled his report to New York, "I did not sleep a wink all the way over, and while I may look a bit fagged, I am fit enough to fly on to Novo-Sirbirsk." Wiley bragged on the *Winnie Mae,* "She's behaved loyally and bravely so far. She's built for speed, power and economy, and even the mechanics at Tempelhof Airdrome marveled at her fit condition after my hard drive across the Atlantic. Not a single gadget was out of order."[195]

After a two-hour delay in Berlin, Wiley took off for Novosibirsk, Russia, and he began having problems with the Sperry autopilot. He also discovered that several of his maps of Russia were missing, so he turned back to land at Koenigsberg, the capital city of East Prussia. The name of the city was later changed to Kalingrad when East Prussia became part of the Soviet Union. The problem with the autopilot was a leak in the oil supply line to the servo unit. Wiley had to manually fly "blind" using the gyroscopes in the autopilot. It took him four and a half hours to fly the 340 miles, an average speed of only 78 miles an hour.

More problems developed with the autopilot when Wiley arrived at Koenigsberg, and heavy clouds grounded him for the night. His bad eye socket was irritated and bothering him greatly so he found a local doctor who treated the socket with boric acid, then he slept for six hours and began fresh the next day.

Wiley was behind schedule and wondered out loud to reporters in Koenigsberg if he should fly directly to Novosibirsk, as scheduled, or stop in Moscow where mechanics were available to repair the autopilot. He wanted to break his previous record, but he wanted even more just to complete the solo around the globe. He decided to be on the safe side and stop in Moscow. He left Koenigsberg in such a hurry that he forgot his suitcase. He flew five hours through rain and clouds to Moscow.

Wiley took Moscow by surprise. Only a hundred people were at the airport when his white and purple monoplane "flashed across the field from the southwest, circled and swooped down, then with a big bump touched the ground." Three doctors examined Wiley and found him to be in surprisingly good condition, showing no signs of fatigue. One of the Russian doctors with twelve years' experience in aviation medicine said he had never met a pilot with such "steady, solid nerves and such a regular pulse" after such an exhausting flight.[196]

Wiley waited patiently in Moscow as mechanics repaired the leaking oil lines to the autopilot. He was already a day behind schedule, less than halfway through the trip. Wiley got a haircut and a shave and explained to a *New York Times* correspondent in

Moscow that he was not tired and that "any American pioneer could do without sleep for a week."[197] Wiley ate a light meal and studied weather reports provided by the Russian government that had set in motion a plan to broadcast English weather information every ten minutes to Wiley from Kazan, Sverdlovak, Omsk and Novosibirsk.

While in Moscow Wiley learned of the deaths of two Lithuanian fliers who were attempting a trans-Atlantic flight. Captain Stephen Darious and Stanley Girenas were killed upon impact when their plane crashed in a forest in the Pomeranian region of Germany. Peasant women gathering mushrooms found the shattered wreckage and bodies of the two men.

The plane had hit the edge of the forest, slid along the treetops for more than 200 feet, then smashed into the ground. The motor and propeller were "deeply buried in the soil." The rest of the machine was a "tangled mass of wood and wire."[198]

The same thunderstorm that had knocked out instruments on the *Winnie Mae* and forced Wiley to land at Koenigsberg, caused the Lithuanians to lose their way. When they ran out of gas, their plane plummeted to the earth.

News of the deaths of Darious and Girenas and the crash of Mattern resulted in sleepless nights for Mae and Wiley's parents back in Maysville.

Soon word came from the Russian mechanics working on the *Winnie Mae* that the plane was ready to go. At 5:10 P.M. the motor roared, small boys who stood in awe of the plane were shooed away by sentries, and Wiley sailed away from Moscow over the trees at the end of the runway, "made a wide half circle gleaming like a seagull and disappeared at a terrific speed."

It was a stressful, 13-hour-and-15-minute flight from Moscow to Novosibirsk. Wiley almost scraped the top of a hill as he flew through fog and rain and had to negotiate his way through a pass in the Ural Mountains that were 6,000 feet higher than he was flying. Wiley later said if he had had a parachute on the *Winnie Mae*, he would have jumped out two or three times rather than risk the flight through the mountains. For brief periods, he climbed to

21,000 feet to get above the bad weather. Wiley knew how long he could endure the lack of proper oxygen at high altitudes, and always brought the *Winnie Mae* back to a lower altitude before his physical functions were affected. Wiley had more mechanical problems.

The automatic pilot feed pipe became disconnected again—not that it mattered much because the mountains constituted a greater danger than the loss of the ability to fly automatically. Instead of 11 hours Wiley estimated for the trip between Moscow and Novosirbirsk, it took him over 13. "Dead reckoning" among the mountains was a real strain.[199]

Wiley became disoriented on his way to Novosibirsk. Cold air made him drowsy and his lungs ached with the need for more oxygen. He decided to find out exactly where he was and landed beside a mountain highway. Two peasants came along, but Wiley could not understand them or make them understand him. Finally, with the use of sign language, one peasant said Novosibirsk was 300 miles to the west, the other said the town was 1,500 miles to the east. Wiley took off and guessed correctly that he was still west of Novosibirsk. He soon broke out of the bad weather and picked up the railroad tracks again.

Waiting for Wiley at Novosibirsk was Fay Gillis, the daughter of an American engineer who was in Russia building zinc plants. Fay was the aviation reporter in the Soviet Union for the *New York Herald Tribune.* She had been a pilot since age 19, spoke fluent Russian, and had offered her services to Wiley as an interpreter for his refueling stop at Novosibirsk. Wiley had sent Fay a cable from New York:

LIKE YOU ARRIVE NOVOSIBIRSK BY JULY FIRST, ARRANGE, GAS PLANE IN TWO HOURS WHILE I SLEEP, THEN FLY WITH ME TO KHABAROVSK TO DIRECT SERVICE THERE [STOP] GET ME BEST MAPS NOVOSIBIRSK TO KHABAROVSK [STOP] WILL PAY YOUR EXPENSE [STOP] REGARDS [STOP] WILEY POST. [200]

Wiley's New York agent, Lee Trenholm, later canceled the promised flight of Fay from Novosibirsk to Khabarovsk because the dual pilots would defeat Wiley's attempt at a "solo" around the earth. Nevertheless, Fay was a great help at Novosibirsk for the two hours Wiley stayed there. He refueled and took to the air, without eating a meal. Fay sent a cable to Mae Post at Wiley's headquarters at the Roosevelt Hotel in New York:

WILEY BEEN AND GONE. ONLY STAYED TWO HOURS AND A HALF. HE'S IN HIGH SPIRITS DESPITE BAD LUCK WITH WEATHER. EXPECTS TO BE IN NEW YORK IN THREE DAYS. HAVE FUN.[201]

More problems plagued Wiley's trip toward Khabarovsk. The automatic pilot malfunctioned again and Wiley was forced to land at Irkutsk. However, he averaged over 161 miles an hour on the 1,055 mile leg, his fastest leg of the entire trip. He had arrived at Irkutsk 16 and a half hours ahead of the pace of the 1931 record flight, but now was only three hours ahead.

Russian weathermen warned Wiley of an approaching storm over the Baikal Mountains so Wiley stayed in Irkutsk several hours. He again took off, headed to Khabarovsk. He followed the Trans-Siberian Railroad at a speed of almost 200 miles an hour, helped by a strong tailwind. Then darkness and rain closed in on Wiley and another unscheduled landing, this time at Rukhlovo, had to be made.

Wiley was terribly thirsty when he landed at Rukhlovo and had an animated discussion with his Russian hosts that he wanted "water," not Russian liquor. He settled for a glass of tea. Wiley would not get his "glass of water" until he arrived in Alaska. Later Will Rogers would quip that Wiley "left two bottles of vodka and flew 1,800 miles for a drink of water. . . 'Course, if it had been me I would have poured one bottle in my engine and the other in me, and I would have been in New York by sundown."

After a few hours on the ground at Rukhlovo, Wiley flew the remaining four and a half hours to Khabarovsk.

Jimmy Mattern had been Wiley's competitor until a few days before. Now, Jimmy, who was still resting up in Russia before going home to America, helped the Russians prepare weather reports for Wiley's use.

Wiley was tired as he left Khabarovsk for the grueling, 3,100-mile trip to Fairbanks, Alaska. This time, there was no Gatty to share his feelings with, there was only the drone of the Wasp engine. The trek from Khabarovsk to Fairbanks was a tremendous challenge for a fresh pilot, much less a fatigued pilot who had flown more than half way around the earth already.

For seven hours Wiley plunged into the clouds across the Sea of Okhotsk and flew by instruments and autopilot. When the clouds disappeared, Wiley broke out over the Gulf of Anadyr. Hours rolled by as the *Winnie Mae* flew over the Bering Strait, and then Wiley saw the outline of the Seward Peninsula. The coast of Alaska was in sight and Wiley dropped altitude.

When mountains began to appear again above the clouds, Wiley knew he had crossed Bering Strait and was above Alaska. He had crossed the narrow stretch of water between Russia and Alaskan territory "without even a fleeting glimpse of the surface." He flew to the north side of the mountains, where the wind had blown the clouds away, dropped down low, and flew back to the coast. He followed the coast around Cape Prince of Wales to Nome, where he circled the radio station and the airport, then headed for Fairbanks.

The clouds were low and the visibility poor. He decided to "climb back on top." He was unable to pick up radio signals from Fairbanks and began what turned out to be a "1,200-mile-wandering" around the central part of Alaska.

For seven hours he dodged mountains, including 20,000 foot Mt. McKinley, and followed rivers "to no avail." He was completely lost. He headed back toward the coast of Nome and on the way spied a village below. He later found out the town was called Flat.[202]

During Wiley's wandering, veteran bush pilots Noel and Ada Wien spotted the *Winnie Mae* circling over the Yukon River as if

Mae Post kept in contact with Wiley during his 1933 solo flight by receiving daily telegrams. Courtesy *The Daily Oklahoman.*

lost. They tried to fly close to Wiley to get his attention, but failed. The Vega was much faster than their Bellanca aircraft so Wiley soon was out of sight.

In McGrath, Alaska, radio operator Oscar Winchell saw the *Winnie Mae* fly over and knew that Wiley was off his scheduled route for Fairbanks. Winchell unsuccessfully tried to raise Wiley on the radio.

When Wiley saw the airport at the small mining settlement of Flat, he decided to land. He was 31 hours ahead of his 1931 record and physically was in no condition to continue. He trimmed back the *Winnie Mae* and prepared to land.

CRASH LANDING AT FLAT

I kept figuring every minute I better fasten my parachute.

WILEY POST

THE FLAT, ALASKA, airport was nothing but a crude landing strip. When Wiley gently set the *Winnie Mae* down at Flat, 300 miles southwest of Fairbanks, the landing seemed normal, for a moment. The plane rolled down the grass strip until Wiley saw a ditch. He was unable to stop in time and the *Winnie Mae* skidded into the ditch.

She lurched over on her right wing, and right leg of her landing gear crumpled. Her tail came up, "driving her nose into the earth," bending the complex Smith propeller. She finally came to a stop with her engine cowl stuck in the dirt.[203]

After being helped out of his plane, Wiley was taken to the nearby hangar and examined for injuries. None were found. The crash was similar to the accident that he and Gatty had at Solomon, Alaska on the 1931 flight. The damage looked repairable so Wiley called his old friend, Joe Crosson, a bush pilot who was chief pilot for Pacific Alaska Airways in Fairbanks. Crosson and three other mechanics left immediately for Flat with a replacement propeller and temporary landing gear for the *Winnie Mae*.

While Crosson was in the air, Wiley got some much-needed sleep. Workers at a nearby mining company built a tripod derrick of large timbers and lifted the airplane with a block and tackle. The plane was ready for Crosson and his crew to repair the landing gear and propeller. When Crosson arrived, Wiley showed him what needed to be done, and Wiley went back to sleep.

Bright and early the next morning the *Winnie Mae* was ready to go. Wiley flew alongside Crosson on the trip to Fairbanks for refueling. Bad weather over Canada further delayed the trip. For eight long hours Wiley sat at Weeks Field, the small airport at Fairbanks.

Taking off from Fairbanks, Wiley began a tense nine hours to Edmonton, Alberta. He averaged more than 154 miles an hour on the leg, even though he flew through heavy clouds by instrument for more than half the trip. It was a dangerous leg, for many mountains above 15,000 feet lay in northern Canada. Several times Wiley spotted mountains and climbed to 20,000 feet, near man's limit in an unpressurized cabin.

Wiley was flying at 21,000 feet over the mountains, in a chilly air with temperature of six degrees below zero. He later recalled the event as the most frightening moment of the trip: "Ice was forming on my ship and forcing me down at the rate of 100 feet a minute. I had the motor wide open, but still I could not get an air speed above 125 miles and I kept going down. I knew the mountains came up to 15,000 feet there, and if I ever had got down to 16,000 feet I would be gone. I kept figuring every minute I had better fasten my parachute."[204]

Wiley dropped into Edmonton almost 11 hours ahead of his 1931 pace. It was raining cats and dogs as he set the *Winnie Mae* down. Despite the early hour a crowd had gathered to watch for his plane. About 6:00 A.M. the *Winnie Mae* was sighted. Wiley circled the airport twice. The rain cloud was so dense that he disappeared for a time to the east. People who had waited at the airport all night for a glimpse of Wiley feared for a moment that he would continue eastward, but soon he returned and landed.

Wiley was tired and "suffering from a severe headache" when he arrived. Mayor D. K. Knott, who had waited three hours at the airport, welcomed Wiley who "thanked everyone with a smile, but could not hide his weariness."[205]

At Edmonton, Wiley was only 2,000 miles from his final destination of New York City. He was in a hurry, but problems encountered while he refueled the *Winnie Mae* cost him 90 minutes.

This time the Edmonton Field was dry, so Wiley was able to make an ordinary takeoff, and the citizens of Edmonton were deprived of seeing the *Winnie Mae* "roar down Portage Avenue again."[206]

Wiley left Edmonton for the final stretch home. He was more fatigued than ever before in his life. He let his autopilot do the flying and tried to rest. Wiley allowed himself to doze from time to time. To make sure that he would do more than doze, he rigged his "Rube Goldberg" by tying a wrench to his finger with a piece of string. He held the wrench in his hand and whenever he slipped off into a sleep deep enough to relax the hand, the wrench "fell, jerked his finger, and woke him up."[207]

The *Winnie Mae* was now on a downhill run, across Canada, over the Great Lakes, and into the United States. The many commercial broadcast stations in America allowed him to use his ADF to fly a perfect course. Wiley heard live radio broadcasts from New York City estimating his time of arrival. For the next few hours and days, the entire world would bestow upon Wiley an unprecedented shower of genuine appreciation for his heroic efforts.

AMERICA WELCOMES
HER HERO

Wiley Post

The airplane was engulfed by a swarm of humanity—

NEW YORK TIMES

FIFTY THOUSAND PEOPLE jammed Floyd Bennett
Field in New York City under the cover of darkness July
22, 1933. It was as if the world had stopped for this
moment in history.

As the *Winnie Mae* neared New York, "a great popular clamor"
began to fill the radio airwaves. "Extras" flooded the city's news-
stands in anticipation of Wiley's return. Some newspapers por-
trayed him as a "one-eyed superman," who could fly an airplane as
if he had mystical powers. One reporter stated that Wiley was part
American Indian, while another described him as a tough South-
westerner who could use a tomahawk as well as any Indian, nei-
ther statement was true.[208]

Mae, who lost about as much sleep as Wiley did on the flight, was ready for her flying husband to come home. The *New York Times* reported:

> In her smart blue ensemble she tripped through the corridor of the hotel and started for the flying field. She did not know it, but a brand new automobile was awaiting her there, a coupe her husband had purchased before starting on his flight and which he had arranged to present to her as a surprise on his return. She was to drive him away from the field in the new car after his landing.[209]

For awhile, airport officials thought fog might cause Wiley to divert his landing to another airport. Airport offices were swamped with telephone calls from people wanting to know what time Wiley would arrive. Soon the fog moved out of the area and New Yorkers were ready for the big moment.

At ten minutes until midnight, the sound of the *Winnie Mae's* engine could be heard to the west of the airport. Then, her landing lights appeared upon the horizon. Wiley sat the plane down softly on the runway as the gigantic crowd exploded.

When Wiley taxied the *Winnie Mae* up to the floodlit terminal buildings, the airplane was "engulfed by a swarm of humanity." About 600 policemen had been sent to handle the throngs that swarmed over the airport, but it is doubtful if 1,600 would have been enough. 5,000 automobiles jammed the airport's parking facilities, spilling over into vacant lots nearby and the roads leading out of Brooklyn and Queens to Floyd Bennett Field were a "hopeless tangle of snarled traffic."[210]

Another newspaper account said:

> Then someone in the crowd spotted the white fuselage. A cry went up: "Here he is!" And like a vast tidal wave the crowd rushed forward, sweeping past the police, over the fence and out upon the field.[211]

Wiley raised himself through the hatch on the top of the plane and viewed the cheering masses. His white eye patch was dirty and he quickly borrowed a handkerchief to cover his bad eye. Wiley

Wiley arrived at Floyd Bennett Field (now John F. Kennedy Airport) just before midnight on July 22, 1933, the first person to ever fly alone around the earth. He climbed from the cockpit of the Winnie Mae to a hero's welcome of more than 50,000 people. Radio reporters and photographers rushed the airplane to record one of history's greatest moments. Courtesy the Associated Press, Wiley Post Collection, Oklahoma Historical Society.

tied the white handkerchief around his head and met his admiring public, wife Mae, Harold Gatty, Leslie Fain, and a number of Oklahomans, including Walter Harrison, John Kroutil, William Bell Huggins Jr., Thomas S. Hanna Jr., Chauncey D. Nicolls, Bennie Turner, and "Red" Gray. The scene was sheer chaos.

After several wild minutes, "while the crowd jammed in around the *Winnie Mae*," Wiley was finally able to get out of the airplane only by crawling back over the wing to its trailing edge, where he slid to the ground. He made his way to a waiting car.

Meanwhile, the Navy sent a detail of men in to surround the *Winnie Mae* to protect her from souvenir hunters. She was eventu-

Around the World Solo Flight
7 days 18 hours 49 mins
Wiley Post
7/22/33

Wiley poses with his beloved *Winnie Mae* after his solo trip around the world, July, 1933. Courtesy Oklahoma Historical Society.

ally rolled off "to the protection of a Navy hangar." It was the ugly custom of souvenir hunters to almost literally tear an airplane to pieces in their frantic desire for a piece of fabric from it. Fortunately for the *Winnie Mae* she was 90 percent plywood.[212]

Reporters from all over the world had a thousand questions for Wiley, who said he was all right, except for a terrible headache from flying at high altitudes. He was obviously tired, "but not as tired as when Gatty and I did this thing two years ago." Wiley summed up the trip by saying, "I have tried to make this flight with the idea of not killing myself, not only because I did not want to get killed, but because it would look bad for aviation." The celebration lasted at the airport until 3:00 A.M. when Wiley finally went with Mae to the Hotel Roosevelt.

Wiley had broken his old around-the-world record by more than 21 hours. He had circled the earth in seven days, 18 hours, 49½ minutes, with a total flying time of 115 hours, 36½ minutes.

Wiley's record was unique among all records in the history of aviation. He was the first person to fly around the earth twice and the first to make the flight alone. Even though his record was broken 14 years later, it was done with far superior aircraft and under totally different conditions.

It was as if the nation could not do enough to show its respect for Wiley's feat. He was without a doubt the nation's reigning hero. The *New York Times* recognized the historically significant contribution made by Wiley's flight around the world:

> By winning a victory with the use of gyrostats, a variable pitch propeller, and a radiocompass, Post definitely ushers in a new stage of long-distance aviation. The days when human skill alone and an almost bird-like sense of directions enabled a flier to hold his course for long hours through a starless night or over a fog are over. Commercial flying in the future will be automatic.[213]

Wiley was visited at the Hotel Roosevelt the next day by General Italo Balbo, the Italian flier who had led an armada of airplanes from Italy, across the Atlantic, to the United States. General Balbo, "immaculate in his gold-starred white uniform," told Wiley, with Latin grace, that none but a man like Wiley could have made the flight around the world, almost without sleep, in a time under eight days and against every imaginable obstacle. Wiley, "looking the rough-and-ready flier he is," in a business suit, soft blue shirt and oil-soaked shoes he wore around the world, naively confessed to Balbo that he thought most generals were "phony" but that Balbo was the real thing.[214]

Doctors checked Wiley over and found he had lost eight pounds and had slept less than a day of the previous week. He had little appetite and had only orange juice for breakfast and a club sandwich and bottle of beer for dinner. He left the hotel only to check on the *Winnie Mae* and retrieve some items from the plane.

"POST PREDICTS 48-HOUR FLIGHTS AROUND WORLD WITHIN FEW YEARS," read the headline on page two of the *New York Times* on July 2. Wiley wrote a memorable follow-up story to his flight, "After my second experience flying around the world, I be-

After another record ticker-tape parade in New York City, Wiley was honored on the steps of City Hall. He was lauded by New York Mayor John P. O'Brien (left). Mae (right) made every appearance with Wiley and was called by the press "the most supportive of wives." Courtesy Oklahoma Historical Society.

lieve there is almost no limit to the quickness with which that journey eventually can be made."[215]

Wiley was the guest at a luncheon sponsored by the Aeronautical Chamber of Commerce at the Hotel Roosevelt. The organization's president, Thomas Morgan, described Wiley's flight as "writing a whole new volume in the history of aviation." In a ten-minute speech, long for Wiley, he thanked the aviation community for its support. Amelia Earhart and Harold Gatty joined Mae Post as other special guests at the luncheon.

Mayor John P. O'Brien rolled out New York's red carpet. Wiley's second ticker-tape parade was larger than in 1931. A squad of policemen on horses and motorcycles, sirens screaming, escorted Wiley and Mae to Battery Park for the start of the parade that traveled up Broadway to City Hall. Eighteen thousand people were on hand to see the parade begin. Plans to pull the *Winnie Mae* in the parade were scrapped because officials feared the wings of the plane were too wide and might cause injury to the tens of thousands of people who lined New York's streets.

With "a white patch covering his bad eye" Wiley rode up Broadway beside Philip D. Hoyt, First Deputy Police Commissioner, and chairman of the Mayor's reception committee. Ticker

Safely back in
their hotel room
at the Roosevelt
Hotel in New
York, Wiley
shows Mae the
route he flew
from Siberia to
Alaska on his trip
around the earth.
Courtesy of *The
Daily
Oklahoman.*

President Franklin Roosevelt welcomed Wiley to the White House to personally thank him for his "courage and stamina" in flying alone around the world in the *Winnie Mae. Courtesy The Daily Oklahoman.*

tape, and for the sake of novelty, tiny parachutes, floated down upon him while thousands cheered.[216]

Mayor O'Brien pinned a new gold medal on Wiley's coat and read enthusiastic words from a prepared manuscript. O'Brien said Wiley's two flights around the world had made him "a symbol of man's triumph over the elements," and compared Wiley with Magellan and Drake.

The next day Wiley and Mae traveled by train to Washington, D. C. to visit the White House and President Franklin D. Roosevelt. The President expressed the gratitude of an entire nation for Wiley's courage and physical endurance. After a reception at the National Press Club, Wiley and Mae returned to New York.

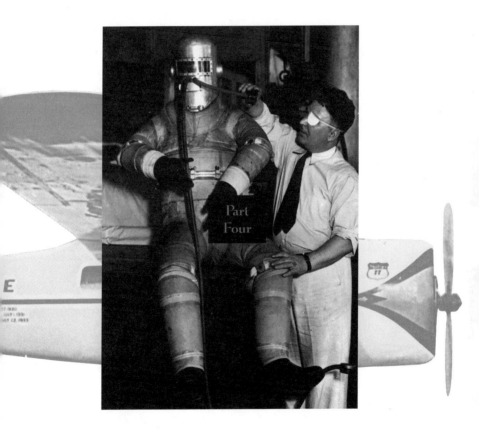

Part
Four

AHEAD OF HIS TIME

It takes healthy nerves to fly around the world alone—

ILEY HARDLY HAD TIME to rest up from his globe-circling trip before he was predicting unimaginable feats in aviation. The July 30, 1933 edition of the *New York Times* carried a special story about Wiley's prediction that airplanes could someday fly 500 to 600 miles an hour:

> Post is deadly serious about it. He wants to experiment with the Winnie Mae, the plane with which he has twice set new marks around the world... His last trip convinced him, he says, of the practical possibility of world circuits in about two days in planes with supercharged engines, sealed cabins, and controllable pitch propellers... With such equipment the stocky, one-eyed Oklahoma flier does not believe 500 miles an hour impossible for his famous plane 'up where the air is thin.' [217]

Wiley's 1933 flight advanced aviation beyond the general public's imagination. His use of the Sperry autopilot allowed pilots to use the "robot" to fly specific headings and eliminate the old requirement of a flier gripping the controls at every moment of flight. The radio homing device received its first real test on long flights, relieving the strain of continual hand navigation computations.

Wiley was awarded the Harmon Trophy for excellence in aviation in August, 1934. He is congratulated by former trophy winner James (Jimmy) Doolittle. Courtesy Wide World Photos and *The Daily Oklahoman.*

Wiley stands in the cockpit of the *Winnie Mae* that was towed to a vacant lot adjacent to Rockefeller Center in Manhattan where people could pay $1.00 for a closer look at the famous airplane. Fifth Avenue is just beyond the back fence. Wiley appeared at the nearby Radio City Music Hall and told audiences of the challenges and danger of his solo around the world. Courtesy The Associated Press and *The Daily Oklahoman.*

One of the greatest advances was Wiley's use of a small heater on the exhaust of the *Winnie Mae's* engine that recirculated the warm air to the cylinders, maintaining a constant engine temperature regardless of the altitude or outside temperature, an innovation that would make it possible to fly in the stratosphere. Despite expected difficulties flying in "thin air," he predicted that circling the globe within two days was possible. Within five years, Howard Hughes and a crew of four flew around the earth in three days, 19 hours, and eight minutes.[218]

In the summer of 1933, Wiley picked up numerous honors for his solo flight around the world. He received hundreds of invitations to speak at banquets and dedicate airports. He received the Gold Medal of the Federation Aeronautique Internationale, awarded annually to the person in the world who contributed most to aviation. Charles Lindbergh was the only other American to previously win the award. Wiley also won the Harmon International Trophy, given by the League of International Aviators.

Wiley certainly made more money out of the 1933 flight than his flight with Gatty in 1931. Even though he did not smoke, he signed a contract to appear in a magazine ad for Camel cigarettes. The ad said, "It takes healthy nerves to fly around the world alone." Wiley made money by selling his story to magazines and endorsing Mobil gasoline and Sperry gyroscopes. He received several thousand dollars by promoting the products of the Socony Vacuum Company on a national tour.

Wiley accepted, over the objection of friends like Harry Frederickson, an invitation to appear at a series of aviation lectures at the Radio City Music Hall in New York. He showed newsreels of the flight and related interesting stories of his travels. On a vacant lot next to the Rockefeller Center, still under construction in 1933, Wiley displayed the *Winnie Mae*. Large crowds paid a dollar for an up-close look at the famous plane. Capacity crowds showed up to see Wiley, but his dreams of making $40,000 in the deal vanished. He cleared less than $7,000.

Frederickson had objected to Wiley's appearance at the Radio City Music Hall as "demeaning" to Wiley's status as an aviator.

Will Rogers came to Wiley's defense:

> Say, after what that little guy went through with, nobody
> should criticize him even if he turned banker or took a seat on
> the stock exchange.[219]

In a Kiwanis Club speech in Quincy, Illinois, in September,
Wiley predicted that "regular transoceanic service" was not far off.
He narrowly escaped death the next day when he experienced engine failure while taking off from the Quincy airport. The *Winnie
Mae* landed in a heavily wooded area and was scarred and battered
by the crash landing. Wiley suffered only cuts and bruises but was
admitted to the local hospital for observation.

George Brauer of Braniff Airways flew to Quincy to help Wiley
bring the plane back to Oklahoma City for repairs. Brauer made a
grim discovery, someone had dumped five gallons of water in the
Winnie Mae's fuel tanks. It was not the first, nor the last attempt
to sabotage Wiley's airplanes.

Back in Oklahoma City, Brauer and his staff of mechanics at
Braniff restored the *Winnie Mae* to her original condition. Once
Wiley got out of the hospital, he turned his attention to his next
project—testing the "thin air," the stratosphere.

Wiley had spent his career behind the controls of an airplane
trying to fly farther and faster around planet earth. He had conquered the horizontal—now he looked up—vertically. He knew
the key to the future of fast airplanes and world-wide mail and
passenger service was in the upper levels of air, a hostile world
where man could not live without special equipment. Wiley Post
was the man with the dream and the inspiration to explore that
unknown world.

THE THIN AIR

If I get popped off, that's the way I want to go—

WILEY POST

ILEY KNEW that the next leap in aviation was in high altitude flying. He was America's lone voice in predicting regular flights above 30,000 feet in the stratosphere, the upper layer of the earth's atmosphere that is almost completely free of clouds and elements of weather. The one special characteristic of the stratosphere that intrigued Wiley was the fast streams of air he called "high winds." Today, we know the natural flow of air as jet streams. Wiley Post, more than anyone else in history, tested, proved and gave notoriety to jet streams and high altitude flying.

Wiley was, of course, not the first person to wonder about the jet stream. In 1850 American balloonist John Wise had talked about "the great river of air."[220] In 1931, Swiss physicist Auguste Piccard attracted worldwide attention when he made the first balloon ascension into the stratosphere, reaching an altitude of almost 52,000 feet.

Ironically, it was the promise of a $50,000 prize in a 1934 race from England to Australia, a race that he would never actually enter, that provided the impetus for Wiley to develop the pressurized flying suit. The MacRobertson Race was planned for October, 1934, and was created by Sir John MacRobertson to celebrate the centennial of Melbourne, Australia, and publicize the availability of air travel to Australia.

In 1935 Wiley agreed to fly experimental air mail flights. R.C. Jopling, left, public relations director for Phillips Petroleum Company, Wiley, and TWA president Jack Frye look over the final contract outlining details of the cooperative venture between TWA and Phillips to test the commercial possibilities of stratosphere flying. Courtesy Corporate Archives, Phillips Petroleum Company.

After signing a contract with Frank Phillips, Wiley added a "Phillips 77" decal to the fuselage of the *Winnie Mae*. Courtesy Oklahoma Historical Society.

Below left: It was Billy Parker (right), chief of aviation for Phillips Petroleum Company who talked Wiley into flying for Phillips in 1934. Courtesy Corporate Archives, Phillips Petroleum Company

Wiley recognized that he could not win the 12,500 mile race with the *Winnie Mae* unless he made substantial modifications. His only chance was to fly above 30,000 feet and take advantage of the jet stream in parts of the world where he could calculate its direction and velocity. There was a problem, however. The *Winnie Mae* was built primarily from plywood and could not be pressurized. If Wiley could not pressurize his plane, his only alternative was to pressurize himself.

The U.S. Army had attempted pressurization of a bi-plane as early as 1920 when a glass windshield was built into the side of a steel tank which was pressurized. The experiment flopped when the pilot experienced severe ear pains and was barely able to land the airplane.[222]

It was Wiley's aeronautical genius that birthed the radical concept of a pressurized flying suit to be worn by a pilot on high altitude flights. It was impractical to pressurize the *Winnie Mae* because of its plywood and wire construction. So Wiley conceived

Wiley's association with Frank Phillips was brief but very public. The public relations department of Phillips Petroleum Company posed Wiley by Phillips 66 and Phillips 77 signs at every opportunity and invited camera-ready photographers. Courtesy Corporate Archives, Phillips Petroleum Company.

the design and construction of a pressure suit for flight. He planned to have the suit tailored to his body. He saw no reason why he could not exceed 250 miles an hour in the "thin air" high above the earth.[223]

In early 1934, Wiley called his old friend Jimmy Doolittle, who had become director of aviation for the Shell Oil Company. Doolittle pledged to keep secret Wiley's plans to build a pressure suit and referred him to the B. F. Goodrich plant in Los Angeles. In June Wiley visited the Goodrich plant and ordered "a rubber suit" that would be pressurized by means of compressed air created by a supercharger attached to the *Winnie Mae*'s engine.

Wiley asked Goodrich to construct the suit so that oxygen could be piped to the pilot from tanks of liquid oxygen, certainly a novel idea for 1934. At a cost of only $75, Goodrich test scientists built a suit from rubberized parachute material that made the flier look like "a man from Mars." A metal belt sealed the top half of the suit to the bottom half. A rectangular plastic vision plate allowed the flier to see out of the aluminum helmet. Pigskin gloves protected his hands and rubber boots covered his feet.

A bulge was located over each ear of the helmet to accommodate headphones and a small door was placed over the mouth. When the suit was unpressurized, breathing, speaking, and even eating through the door were possible. Front and back helmet tiedown handles were provided at the lower edges because, when the suit was under pressure, "the helmet tended to rise."[224]

The basic design of Wiley's first pressure suit was sound, but it could not withstand pressures that Wiley would encounter above 27,000 feet. The suit ruptured during a test at the U. S. Army's low-pressure test chamber at Wright Field in Dayton, Ohio, and was discarded. Undaunted, Wiley went back to the drawing table.

The second pressure suit had flexible elbow and knee sections, more comfortable for a pilot spending long hours in flight. In July Wiley, who had gained 20 pounds since 1930, tested the suit himself, but got stuck and the suit had to be cut from him. It was ruined in the process.

The aviation world watched with growing interest Wiley's

progress on the development of a pressure suit. S. E. Perry, Maintenance Superintendent of Braniff Airways said, "Post's plans were so revolutionary . . . that is hard even for the aeronautical engineer or aviation expert to grasp them fully."[225] In August, 1934, Wiley and Russel S. Colley, a Goodrich technical representative, began testing a third and final pressure suit. It had two separate layers, an inner rubber bag that would conform to Wiley's body, and an outer, three-ply cloth suit, made to resist stretching and to hold the rubber suit to Wiley's body. The suit was truly innovative.

The third suit was designed to be entered feet-first through a large neck opening. A totally new helmet was designed "to be bolted in place with wing nuts" after Wiley was in the suit. The helmet seal would be made by two superimposed yokes of flat metal.

In 1934 Phillips Petroleum Company introduced Phillips 77 aviation gasoline. Here Wiley oversees the refueling of his airplane, preparing for a flight to promote the new gasoline brand. Courtesy Corporate Archives, Phillips Petroleum Company.

Since Wiley could not reach the wing nuts in the back of the helmet, he would have to be helped in and out of the suit.[226]

During it first test, the inner layer of rubber held pressure perfectly, but a seam ripped on the outside layer. Two more modifications and elimination of weak-point seams in the crotch area fixed the problem. The new helmet was a creation of science and art.

It had a larger window, which was round and made of glass. The window was left out until Wiley was in flight and ready to pressurize. He would then turn on the oxygen and screw the window in place. Oxygen was brought across the window from the left side to "defog" breath moisture that might precipitate on the glass. This helmet was "wide enough that it accommodated earphones for ADF tuning and voice radio, and it could accommodate a throat microphone."[227]

Largely in secret, Wiley took the world's first and only pressure suit for final testing at Wright Field in August, 1934. The Army considered the tests "classified" and would not comment on sporadic reports in the press about the tests.

On August 27, Wiley made the world's first altitude-chamber test in a flight pressure suit. Mae and several Army Air Corps officials watched the successful test. With his idea and invention fresh, Wiley flew the *Winnie Mae* to Chicago where he was to appear at the World's Fair and attempt to set a world's altitude record. The Pure Oil Company sponsored Wiley's successful attempt on September 5 to reach an altitude of 40,000 feet. The pressure suit worked perfectly, another milestone for the young flier. He now was the first person in history to fly in a pressure suit and the first person to utilize liquid oxygen with a pressure suit.

Wiley was never averse to modifying any equipment he worked with, from the hay rakes on the farm or a 20th-century pressure suit. One of the small changes he made after the Chicago flight was attaching a piece of sponge rubber to the top of the helmet. During the flight, the helmet kept hitting the top of the cockpit, transmitting irritating "bumping noises" to Wiley.

The an. unt of money Pure Oil was willing to devote to high altitude test flights was limited. Wiley shared his concern over the shortage of test money with his friend W. D. "Billy" Parker, manager of the aviation department of Phillips Petroleum Company based in Bartlesville, Oklahoma. Parker, a native of Oklahoma City, was an early pioneer of American aviation. At age 13, he built and flew a pusher-type airplane from a pasture near Ft. Collins, Colorado in 1912. He was granted U. S. pilot license number 44 and joined Phillips Petroleum Company in 1927.

Parker talked to Frank Phillips, president of Phillips Petroleum, about sponsoring Wiley. Phillips had a passion for flying. He had sponsored Hollywood stunt flyer Art Goebel in a race from Oakland, California to Honolulu just three months after Lindbergh's trans-Atlantic flight in 1927. Goebel, flying in a plane called the "Woolaroc" and using Phillips aviation gasoline, won the $25,000 first prize awarded by the Dole Pineapple Company.

Frank Phillips, who knew the value of publicity, latched on to successful aviation heroes such as Goebel to promote his company's aviation fuel. However, in the fall of 1934, Phillips was receiving complaints about the quality of its aviation fuel. Paul Braniff of Braniff Airlines personally complained to Frank Phillips about the aviation fuel burning pistons in two of his planes in one week.

Billy Parker and R. C. Jopling, Director of Public Relations for Phillips Petroleum, advised Frank Phillips that Wiley could generate much-needed publicity for the oil company. Phillips immediately agreed to fund Wiley's continuing experiments in stratospheric flights. A deal was struck between Wiley and Phillips in which Wiley agreed to attempt to break the world altitude record in Bartlesville if Phillips would provide gasoline and oil. Wiley wanted a written guarantee that if he broke the altitude record Phillips would pay him a $1,000 bonus and hire him for $1,500 for two weeks of flying around the country advertising Phillips' new "Phillips 77" aviation gasoline. The "77" came from the gravity of the special blend of aviation fuel. The famous Phillips 66 gasoline for automobiles was named because of its gravity of 66.

Wiley moved his operations to Oklahoma again, and flew the

Winnie Mae to Phillips' headquarters in Bartlesville, ready to attack the altitude record of 47,352 feet, held by Italian Air Force pilot Renato Donati who died less than 24 hours after setting the record. Donati had worn a special helmet over his head but no provision was made to equalize the pressure on his body. Donati set the record on his forty-seventh attempt in a special "trick" plane. Wiley was determined to fly in the stratosphere in a stock model airplane with ordinary aviation gasoline and motor oil.

Phillips mechanic Ernest H. Shultz oversaw modifications to the *Winnie Mae's* engine. The Bendix Company developed an external supercharger or blower that was added to the engine to allow the plane to climb to as high as 50,000 feet. Other changes were made to the aircraft. Since the electric starter motor had been removed, the engine was started "by hand-swinging the propeller." A battery was installed to operate the radio compass, as there was now no electrical system. The wingtip, tail lights and landing lights were removed "to save weight and to decrease drag."[228]

Wiley installed a new carburetor and smaller fuel tanks on the *Winnie Mae*. Phillips' chemists provided high-quality fuel for the experiments.

Ever a businessman, Frank Phillips insisted that Wiley sign a document releasing Phillips Petroleum Company from liability in case Wiley was injured or killed during the high altitude flights. Wiley said, "Sure, I know it's dangerous. If I get 'popped off,' that's the way I want to go, doing the things I want to do."[229]

Lockheed Aircraft Corporation, manufacturer of the *Winnie Mae*, joined Phillips' public relations department in gearing up for a major campaign to promote Wiley's high-altitude flights. Press releases went out to wire services and radio and television networks. Frank Phillips assigned Billy Parker to help Wiley record his observations during the flights. These would be used in magazine articles for the *Saturday Evening Post* and *Collier's*. Wiley prepared mentally for his attempt by quail hunting at Woolaroc with Billy Parker and Bartlesville automobile dealer Bert Gaddis. He planned to carry only 70 gallons of gasoline, giving him less than two hours to climb above 48,000 feet and glide back to earth.

Wiley's first serious attempt at the Donati record came on December 3, 1934. He donned his pressure suit and flew in the stratosphere for two hours, reaching 48,000 feet before an oxygen valve malfunctioned, forcing him to descend and land at Hat Box Field, an army base at Muskogee, Oklahoma, 80 miles southeast of Bartlesville. What Wiley did not know at the time was that he landed 80 miles from where he took off because he was whisked southeastward by the "jet stream."[230] On December 7, Wiley flew for two and a half hours before running out of fuel and gliding back to earth. He wrote about that flight for an aviation yearbook:

> I headed into the wind which I estimated was blowing about 200 miles an hour. From then on I could see without difficulty Oklahoma City 110 miles away and El Reno 150 miles west of my landing field. The thermometer outside registered 70 degrees F. below zero, yet I was comfortable. The flying suit worked perfectly after I had fastened the face-plate of my helmet and turned on the external supercharger at 20,000 feet. They hang floral offerings on good race horses. I would like to hang one on that Wasp engine of mine.[231]

Wiley climbed to 50,000 feet, even though his record could not be confirmed because his altimeter had broken at 35,000 feet. It was the first of at least eight flights Wiley made to 50,000 feet in the *Winnie Mae*. The cold temperatures peeled paint from the plane but its equipment and the world's finest pilot behind the stick combined for man's first view from ten miles up.

The *Wichita Beacon* hailed Wiley for his "magnificent attempt," and Phillips for his "spirit of public service in contributing to the achievements of a man who is making aviation history."

Frank Phillips was uncannily correct in predicting the impact of Wiley's high-altitude flights, "Post has proved to himself and will prove to the world that commercial aviation, at six miles per minute, in altitudes from 30,000 to 50,000 feet, is a definite reality, with practical equipment."

TRANSCONTINENTAL
FLIGHTS

That guy don't need wheels—

WILL ROGERS

ILEY TOOK a practical approach to his test flights in 1935, transcontinental flights in the substratosphere. Predictably, flights in the thinner air would substantially cut the time for airplanes to fly coast to coast. The *Winnie Mae* was flown to the Lockheed plant in Burbank, California for modifications to further reduce drag in flight. The standard landing gear was replaced with wheels that were jettisoned after takeoff. The plane then landed on a special landing skid made of spruce.

Transcontinental and Western Airlines (TWA) joined Phillips Petroleum in sponsoring Wiley's efforts. TWA was the second airline to contract with the U.S. Post Office Department to carry mail by air. As part of its sponsorship, TWA required "TWA" and "U.S. Mail" be painted on the side of the *Winnie Mae*. Largely through advances made by Wiley, TWA would become the first airline in the world to use a pressurized cabin in 1940.

Wiley spent a lot of time with oil man Frank Phillips. Wiley and Will Rogers were often the guests of Phillips at his palatial home at Woolaroc, near Bartlesville, "playing poker, rolling dice, and swapping lies" with "Uncle Frank."

Wiley was now answering to two masters, Frank Phillips, and TWA. The airline insisted that he be officially listed as one of their airmail pilots in 1935. Wiley also became a movie star when he appeared in his pressure suit in a Colombia Pictures Corporation movie entitled *Air Fury,* starring Ralph Bellamy. Wiley was paid $350 to play the part of a struggling young airmail company exec-

Wiley made many changes in the *Winnie Mae* during experimental high-altitude flights in 1934. Here the plane is towed by Wiley's car to the repair shop for modifications. Note the addition of the simple landing gear that could be jettisoned after take-off, eliminating drag. Courtesy Oklahoma Historical Society.

Left: Frank Phillips financed Wiley's high-altitude test flights in 1934 and 1935. Phillips poses with Wiley in his "flying suit" at Bartlesville. Courtesy Oklahoma Historical Society.

Facing: Wiley appeared in newspaper and magazine advertisements for Phillips Petroleum. Courtesy Corporate Archives, Phillips Petroleum Company.

Wherever Wiley and the *Winnie Mae* landed, throngs of
people gathered. April 5, 1935. Courtesy The Associated
Press and Oklahoma Historical Society.

Wiley was usually accompanied by a band of reporters and
photographers. Wiley is in the middle of this group in
Bartlesville, 1935. Courtesy Oklahoma Historical Society.

Wiley, in cowboy regalia, relaxes at Frank Phillips' Woolaroc Ranch near Bartlesville in the early summer of 1935. Courtesy Oklahoma Historical Society.

utive who saved the day when he flew the mail from California to New York.

Wiley got into the manufacturing end of the aircraft business in 1935. He was president of the Wiley Post Aircraft Corporation in Oklahoma City. Johnny Burke was manager of the concern that built 13 open-cockpit biplanes. The aircraft was powered by a 40-horsepower converted Model A Ford engine and sold for $1,200. Wiley had earned extra money since 1932 as the Oklahoma and Texas distributor of biplanes built by the Bird Aircraft Corporation of Long Island, New York.

In real life, Wiley loaded up the *Winnie Mae* with 150 pounds of U.S. Mail at Burbank, California, in the early morning hours before dawn on February 22, 1935. With his pressure suit on, he climbed into his plane and headed for New York. The purpose of the trip was to streak across the continent at 375 miles per hour in the thin air of the stratosphere. Arrangements had been made with the National Broadcasting Company stations along the route to broadcast weather reports to Wiley at 30-minute intervals.

With fog and a low ceiling, he took off, jettisoning the landing gear before entering the clouds. Thirty minutes later the engine began throwing oil. It was a dangerous situation. Wiley had 300 gallons of fuel on board and no way to dump it. Calling on his years of flying by the seat of his pants, he landed softly on Muroc Dry Lake in the Mojave Desert, just 57 miles into his flight.

The *Winnie Mae* rolled to within 300 yards of a lone automobile stranded in the desert. H. E. Mertz, who ran the Muroc general store, had had car trouble and his head was under the car's hood when Wiley landed. Wiley's suit was not designed for hiking so Wiley was pretty well worn out by the time he reached Mertz's car. Mertz almost died of fright when Wiley, still in his pressure suit, tapped him on the shoulder to ask for help in getting out of the helmet and suit.

Wiley quickly discovered that it was not a broken oil line that had forced him to make an emergency landing in the desert. Mechanics found a quart of emery dust in the engine, an obvious sabotage attempt.[232]

Wiley and Billy Parker privately told friends that a mechanic had placed the dust in the engine at the request of a disgruntled pilot who was jealous of Wiley. Wiley signed an affidavit that concluded with, "There is no doubt this material was placed there maliciously by some person whose desire was to bring my ship down." There was no official investigation or arrests. The engine had to be completely overhauled.

Will Rogers, who had become increasingly interested in Wiley's flights, was present for the ill-fated February 22 flight:

> Was out at daylight to see Wiley Post take off. Was in the
> camera plane and we flew along with him for about 30 miles.
> We left him at eight thousand feet right over the mountains.
> He soon after had to land. He brought her down on her
> stomach, that guy don't need wheels.[233]

Three weeks later, Wiley was ready to go again. He left Burbank on March 5 and made excellent time until he was about 100 miles east of Cleveland, Ohio, where he ran out of oxygen and had to land. However, the statistics of the flight were phenomenal. He had flown 2,035 miles in the record time of seven hours and 19 minutes, an average ground speed of 279 miles per hour, almost 100 miles per hour more than the maximum air speed of the Wasp engine under normal flying conditions.

Aviation experts hailed the stratospheric flight. The *New York Times* called the Burbank-to-Cleveland flight the "most startling development in aviation since Lindbergh spanned the Atlantic."[234]

Wiley set out again to break the transcontinental record on April 14. However, his external supercharger failed after eight hours and 1,760 miles into the flight and he landed at Lafayette, Indiana. Wiley knew his aging *Winnie Mae* was faltering. His friend Will Rogers suggested to the nation that the plane deserved a final resting place in the Smithsonian Institution and urged the American people to contribute to a fund to allow Wiley to get a new airplane and continue his experiments. In his April 28 column, the humorist Rogers was in fine form:

Wiley Post, just about king of them all, cant break records getting to New York in a six-year-old plane, no matter if he takes it up so high that he coasts in. That Winnie Mae. . . has already done more than any plane in the World. Twice it has broken records clear around the world, broken altitude records. He has thrown off his wheels and has forced landings on his 'Belly.' And she never breaks a thing. So when Wiley gets ready to put her into the Smithsonian we all want to give him a hand.[235]

Despite previous mechanical failures, Wiley tried a fourth transcontinental flight on June 15, 1935. He flew over the Rockies at 35,000 feet. All was well until the Wasp engine threw a piston over the Kansas plains and Wiley landed "dead-stick" at Wichita. The next day he announced that he would retire the *Winnie Mae*.

While Will Rogers had been promoting the *Winnie Mae* for retirement in the Smithsonian, Frank Phillips contemplated buying the plane for permanent display in Bartlesville. But on June 24, 1935, Oklahoma Congressman Josh Lee introduced House Resolution 8622, authorizing the Smithsonian to purchase the *Winnie Mae* for $25,000. Wiley was sad as he parked the plane on the hangar apron at the Bartlesville airport for the last time. Wiley may have worn out an incredible airplane, but he was far from being worn out. His dreams were as high as he thought he could fly.

Even before Wiley put his trusted *Winnie Mae* in mothballs, he began searching for a new aircraft. In February, 1935, he purchased a low-wing "hybrid" airplane, made up of parts from two different airplanes. Wiley bought the plane from Charles H. Babb, a well-known California aircraft broker.

Part of the plane was from a Lockheed Orion that had been flown by TWA for about two years. It had suffered minor damage in two accidents, but was in good shape when Babb bought it from TWA just three days before Wiley showed up. Wiley wanted something different, so he bought an extraordinarily long wing to a Lockheed Explorer from Babb. The Explorer had been badly damaged in an accident in the Canal Zone in 1930.

Babb put the Orion fuselage and the Explorer wing together to create Wiley's new plane. The hybrid carried 270 gallons of gasoline in six tanks. The propeller was a constant-speed Hamilton Standard with three blades. Wiley had some of the *Winnie Mae*'s flight instruments reinstalled in the new airplane that was painted "Waco Red" with a silver stripe.[236]

The press speculated weekly on what Wiley was up to. One paper reported that he and Mae would fly to Siberia in the new plane for a vacation. Another predicted that Wiley, Mae, and Fay Gillis (now Fay Wells, having married well-known news correspondent Linton Wells) would fly to Siberia together, to study the possibility of airmail and passenger routes between Alaska and Russia. The *New York Times* suggested that Pan American Airways had agreed to fund Wiley's search for reasonable routes to Russia, but later changed its mind.[237]

Meanwhile R. C. Jopling, Phillips Petroleum's public relations director, continued to turn out press releases and magazine articles about Wiley. A major New York book publisher, Doubleday, contacted Phillips about contracting with a well-known author to write Wiley's biography. That project was put on hold. Wiley flew to New Jersey in May to visit his old employer Tom Park. He spent a few days trying to convince Park to accompany him to Alaska piloting a second plane as a back-up, on a trip to convince the world that it was practical to fly paying passengers and the mail from Alaska to Russia and beyond. Park decided not to leave his good job as a commercial pilot.

Wiley was still an icon of American folklore. When he and Park went to New York City to "look at some guns and cameras," Wiley was overwhelmed by autograph seekers. Park wrote his sister that "Every time we stopped at a traffic light some yap would jump up on the running board and want Wiley to autograph something. When we went to a cafe the yokels gathered 'round, and refused to be rebuffed." One thing was for sure, Wiley wanted desperately to go to Alaska. Maybe his old friend Will Rogers could help with the costs of the flight. Will had told Wiley that someday he wanted to fly to Siberia.

THE LAST FLIGHT

Me and Wiley are just a couple of Oklahoma boys
trying to get along—

WILL ROGERS

T WAS NO SECRET that not everyone liked Wiley Post.
There had been numerous incidents of sabotage of his aircraft down through the years, any one of which could have
killed him. The sabotage had blemished America's love affair with
Wiley, and his extraordinary skill as a pilot. He often had disagree-
ments with aviation officials, some of them calling him "impossible to deal with" and "big-headed." He was a man on a mission,
and his impatience and quick temper left a few people in his wake
unhappy.

Even though Wiley was admired by millions, he was a very private person. No one knew him better in the ten years before his
death than did Bennie Turner, aviation writer for *The Daily Oklahoman,* who wrote of Wiley:

> He was completely self-contained, so much so that few
> ever knew he was subject to moods, moods that could change
> from blue to rose in a flash. . . It's little traits of personality that
> make a man, a man for friends to enjoy. Little traits like his
> habit of waking in the middle of the night with a desire to walk
> and dressing in the dark so as not to disturb his companions,
> his half anger when anyone worried about him, his dislike of
> liquor yet always eager to mix drinks for others, his love for
> flying yet his devotion to automobiles. . .

From left to right, Joe Crosson, Will Rogers, and Wiley pose for a final time before Will and Wiley left Fairbanks for Point Barrow. The next day Crosson would be called upon to ferry the bodies of his friends on the longest funeral flight in history. Courtesy Oklahoma Historical Society.

Facing page: Wiley's new plane, a hybrid Orion-Explorer. The pontoons were too large for the airplane, a possible cause of the 1935 fatal crash at Point Barrow, Alaska. Courtesy Oklahoma Historical Society.

Below: A graphic summary of Wiley's achievements in aviation. Courtesy Oklahoma Historical Society.

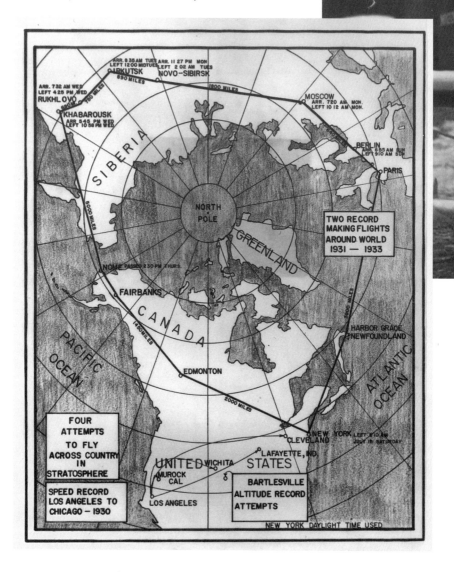

There was nothing sentimental about Post except in regard to children. He was consumed by them. He liked to pick them up, he could never pass a ragged newsboy on the street without buying a paper he did not want... He would sit on the floor for hours and play dolls...

Post had another passion only friends knew. It was for baths. He was always getting dirty and always hating it. When there was something to be done about his plane he would dive in regardless of clothes and help. But as soon as he got within striking distance of a bath he was in it. Four or five baths a day were not unusual.[238]

Will Rogers was "itching" to go to Alaska. As early as March 10, 1935, Will was talking about Alaska and Wiley Post in his daily newspaper column:

I never have been to that Alaska. I am crazy to go up there some time. I would like to go in the Winter, when those old boys are all snowed in, and I could sit around and hear em tell some of those old tales. They do a lot of flying up there. There is some crack aviators. Wiley Post went back up there this last Summer to visit one of them that had helped him out, and they went hunting in a plane... I never did get further north up that way than about a block north of Main Street in Seattle.[239]

On July 25, Wiley, Mae and Will flew to Albuquerque, New Mexico, to spend a few days at Waite Phillips' ranch in the Sangre de Cristo Mountains. It was probably on that trip that Wiley enticed Will to go to Alaska and Siberia with him. Will told the world about their New Mexico vacation:

This sure is a beautiful country up in here, lakes, streams, mountains fish, deer, elk, everything, everytime we would see a good looking ranch and a little meadow down in the canyon Wiley Post would set his Lockheed down in it, visited our old friend Waite Phillips [one of the founders of Phillips Petroleum Company] first, he has a marvelous place, and three hundred twenty five thousand acres of pretty country, now we are at the famous Vermejo Ranch, the greatest fishing and game place in the whole Southwest. Wiley is fishing, and I am out looking at cattle.[240]

Will was tired and needed a long vacation. His latest movie, *Steamboat 'Round the Bend,* had exhausted him and the press reported that he and Wiley were planning a trip to Alaska for him "to rest up." At first Betty Rogers opposed the trip, wanting Will instead to go back east to visit their only daughter Mary who was beginning a stage career. Betty was not so concerned about the trip to Alaska, but the possibility of Wiley and Will going on to Siberia was worrisome to her. Will and Betty had visited Siberia by train a few years before and Betty knew how desolate and primitive that area of the world was. Will wrote later that Betty finally agreed he should go, "When my wife knew it was with Wiley, it dident matter where it was we was going and she was mighty fine about it."[241]

Later news accounts reported that Wiley and Will were actually on a "leisurely two-month trip around the world." Harry G. Frederickson, the Oklahoma City oil man who had been Wiley's close friend for years, told *The Daily Oklahoman* that he had visited with Wiley and Will before they left California. Will was completely funding the trip and had described the trip to Frederickson, "Well, we got all the time we want. When we feel like flying we'll take a little hop. When we feel like sitting, we'll just sit and visit awhile."[242]

Wiley renewed his passport in San Francisco in late July and flew his Orion-Explorer to Seattle on August 1 to be fitted with pontoons for landing on the waters of Alaska. The plane had no official name even though Wiley sometimes called it "Aurora Borealis," after the northern lights. Will called the aircraft "Post Toasty" and other people called it less complimentary names such as "Wiley's Orphan" or "Wiley's Bastard."

The pontoons that Wiley had ordered for the plane did not arrive in Seattle on time. Wiley settled for another set, made for a much larger airplane. Rumors in the press now had Wiley, Mae, and Will making the trip. For some reason, Mae decided not to go. When Will flew to Seattle on August 4, he wrote, "Mrs. Post decided at the last minute to go up to Alaska a few days later by boat, so it's only Wiley and I that are taking off. Ship looks mighty pretty. It's a bright red with a few trimmings of White stripes. The pontoons are awful big looking things but Wiley says 'None Too Big.' "[243]

Wiley removed one of the seats in the Orion-Explorer to make more room for luggage and supplies. He packed a rubber boat, a canoe paddle, life vests, fishing rods and reels, coils of rope, and his gun case, since he planned to spend some time hunting in Alaska. For Will, they loaded two cases of chili so he "would have something good to fall back on in case we couldn't find any good home cookin."

During his final trip to Alaska in August, 1935, Wiley downed a Kodiak bear on a hunting trip near Fairbanks. Courtesy Oklahoma Historical Society.

Wiley and Will Rogers at Aklavik, Alaska, August 11, 1935. Courtesy Oklahoma Historical Society.

The last known photograph of Wiley Post and Will Rogers alive. Will gets ready to climb in the Orion-Explorer while Wiley signs a last autograph at the dock on the Chena River at Fairbanks, Alaska. Courtesy of the Estate of Mrs. D.P. Gustafson and Oklahoma Historical Society.

On the morning of August 6, Wiley and Will prepared to leave Seattle. Will recorded the moment, "Well they've 'bout got the gas in: Wiley is getting nervous. I am anxious to get going too. I think we are going to have a great trip, see lots of country that not too many have seen."[244]

For some unknown reason Wiley and Will dodged the press and their questions about exactly where they were headed. It was not until his newspaper column of August 7 that Will announced he was going "sightseeing" with Wiley. He bragged on Wiley's ability as a pilot and their trip from Seattle to Juneau, "There is millions of channels and islands and bays and all look alike to me but this boy [Wiley] turns up the right alley all the time."

Alaskan pilot Joe Crosson met Wiley and Will at the Juneau airport and escorted them to a local radio station for a live interview show and then on to their night's lodging as a guest of Governor John W. Troy at the Governor's Mansion. Will knew he would be out of touch for awhile so he had written several daily columns in advance and sent them to his newspaper syndicate. Crosson discouraged Wiley from flying north from Juneau because of bad weather, so the two Oklahomans stayed a few days in Juneau.

It certainly appeared that Will was having a great time in Alaska from the freshness of the articles he sent back to American newspapers:

> There aint any unemployed in this country. Thats what the so called idle are doing, is getting autographs, and say they are working 24 hours a day. Fellow comes up and says, 'I see all your pictures' and I ask him which ones, and he cant name a one. Woman brings a little five year old girl up and says, 'Tille wants to meet you, she reads all your little articles in the papers and enjoys em.' Tille says, 'Who is he Ma?'[245]

One of Will's few concerns about the trip seemed to be the presence of sleeping bags in the back of the plane, "Wiley got some sleeping bags; said they was great to sleep in. I never was in one of em. You zip em up around you after you get in em some way. I always have trouble with those zippers, so I can see myself walking around in one of those things all day."[246]

On Friday, August 9, the weather finally cleared in Juneau. Wiley revved up the Orion-Explorer's engine and headed north to Dawson City, in Canada's Yukon Territory. Hundreds of miners gathered at the airport to meet the world celebrities. Wiley was embarrassed when he slipped off a pontoon and fell into the ice-cold water of the Yukon River. Later that day, the "vacationers" flew to Aklavik, a small settlement in the Northwest Territory, to visit with an official of Amtorg, Inc., the Soviet government trading company that had helped Wiley gain permission to land in Russia during his two flights around the world.

Everywhere Wiley and Will went, crowds of interested onlookers congregated. It was Will's first trip to Alaska, but Wiley was

Bush pilot Joe Crosson helps Wiley map out the flight from Fairbanks to Point Barrow, August 15, 1935. Courtesy Oklahoma Historical Society.

well known. Will would flash his famous grin and say, "Me and Wiley are just a couple of Oklahoma boys trying to get along."

On August 11, Will wrote his column from Aklavik, "Eskimos are thicker than rich men at a save-the-Constitution convention. We are headed for famous Herschel Island in the Arctic. Old Wiley had to duck his head to keep from bumping the Arctic Circle as we flew under it."[247]

Will wired Betty a short greeting on August 11: "MOST MARVELOUS TRIP. NO DANGER WITH THIS GUY."

Joe Crosson had flown home to Fairbanks before Wiley and Will arrived on August 12. Joe used hand signals to direct Wiley to a parking spot near the dock on the Chena River. Will was intrigued by the old gold mining town. As usual, a large crowd greeted Wiley and Will.

Will worked the crowd in downtown Fairbanks while Wiley visited with his old friend Crosson. They all had dinner at the Crosson home that night, a night when the idea for the now infamous trip to Point Barrow was born.

Crosson told Will about an interesting man, Charlie Brower, an elderly trader who had spent 50 years around Barrow operating a trading post and whaling station. Will wanted to interview Brower, who was known as "King of the Arctic."

The weather information that Wiley received from the station at Point Barrow made him decide against trying to fly there on August 13. Instead, they flew to Anchorage and made a side trip to fly close to the face of Mt. McKinley, the highest peak in North America.

Point Barrow is 600 miles east of the Bering Strait and is the most northern point of the North American continent. In 1935 the only buildings in the settlement, named by the explorer Beechey in 1826, were the Army Signal Corps station, the government school for Eskimo and Indian children, and the Presbyterian mission and hospital built in 1890. Barrow was home to nine Caucasians and about 500 natives in 1935.

On August 14, the weather was still bad at Barrow so Wiley and Will flew back to Fairbanks to stay all night with Joe Crosson and his family. The next morning, while Will was walking around town, Wiley and Joe looked at houses. Wiley was enamored with Joe's gold mine and everything about Alaska, and thought he and Mae might someday live in Fairbanks. Wiley found a little house on Cushman Street in Fairbanks and rented it. Then he and Joe went to the Fairbanks airport, Weeks Field, and planned a trip to Point Barrow.

Will sent his last telegram to daughter Mary:

> GREAT TRIP. WISH YOU WERE ALONG...GOING TO POINT BARROW TODAY. FURTHEST POINT OF LAND ON WHOLE AMERICAN CONTINENT. LOTS OF LOVE. DON'T WORRY.
>
> DAD

Barrow was ready for Wiley's and Will's visit. The settlement had "no brass bands, no banqueting halls," but did have the choicest reindeer roasts to be had anywhere, "infinitely more juicy and tasty than anything Fairbanks or Nome can produce."[248]

The morning weather reports from Barrow on August 15 were still discouraging, but Wiley decided to take off around 11:30 A.M., hoping the weather would improve. He promised Crosson he would call Barrow for an update later in the afternoon. Wiley and Will flew 40 miles to Harding Lake where it had been prearranged for him to take on extra fuel, having been unable to take off from the Chena River at Fairbanks with a full load of fuel.

There was no telephone at the Harding Lake dock, so Wiley never called Barrow for the latest weather. If he had called, Sergeant Stanley Morgan would have reported dense fog, no ceiling, and no visibility, certainly not flying weather in the vast expanse inside the Arctic Circle.

Wiley had prepared well for his flight to Barrow. He and Joe Crosson had reviewed the latest maps and worked out a preferred route to the outpost.

After flying several hours from Harding Lake, Wiley was lost! It was certainly no time for panic because Wiley had been lost before, in fact lost for seven hours over Alaska during his 1933 trip around the world. He had plenty of fuel and darkness was not a problem since the August sun near the top of the world would not set until almost midnight.

About 3:00 P.M. Gus Massick, a white trader was on his way from his home at Demarcation Point to Barrow in an open motor boat. He distinctly heard a plane overhead, but because of the dense fog, he could not see it. He heard the plane circle and head inland, then return and circle again. Massick plotted his location as about 100 miles southeast of Barrow. The entire coast around Barrow was covered with a thick blanket of fog.

Hours later, Wiley dropped out of the clouds and spotted a small Eskimo hunting camp beside a river. He circled a few more times and picked out a lagoon for a landing strip. He banked the plane toward the smoke that drifted up from the camp. He landed with ease and taxied as close to the shore as he could. Through the fog and drizzle, Wiley and Will crawled out of the plane to ask directions to Point Barrow.

Clair Okpeaha and his family informed Wiley that Barrow was just a few miles to the north. Only about ten minutes after they had arrived at Okpeaha's camp, Wiley restarted the plane's engine and taxied out from the shore, ready for takeoff.

Wiley pushed open the throttle and lifted off the water. As he gave the red airplane more gas and started to bank, the engine sputtered and quit. Within a few seconds the plane nosed into the shallow lagoon and instantly killed its two occupants. The lives of Oklahoma's two most famous citizens had been snuffed out in a horribly tragic moment at the top of the world.

THE WORLD MOURNS

Will Rogers, Wiley Post Die in Airplane Crash in
Alaska; Nation Shocked by Tragedy

THAT *New York Times* headline set the tone for unprecedented news coverage of the deaths of Will Rogers and
Wiley Post. Except during war time, never had American newspapers devoted so much ink to one story. Newspaper editors sent their reporters to get the reaction of public officials, aviators, and the man on the street. The entire world was shocked by
the demise of two of the most popular men on the face of the
earth.

The world first learned about the deaths from a radio message
sent by Sergeant Stanley Morgan from Point Barrow to Seattle.
The message, relayed through two radio stations and received by
Colonel George Kumpe at the Seattle headquarters of the Army
Signal Corps, told how Clair Okpeaha had run 15 miles to Barrow
from the crash scene with the news of the crash. Morgan put together a rescue team, but in his haste, forgot to notify the town's
only physician, Dr. Henry Greist. Morgan and Frank Dougherty, a
local government school teacher, were the only white men who
boarded the open whaleboat full of native men and boys.

Thirty-four-year-old Sergeant Morgan was known as "the law"
at Barrow. He had volunteered for duty when the Army Signal
Corps decided to build a radio station there in 1928, a station
known as "Wamcats," or the Washington-American Military Cable and Telegraph System. Part of Morgan's job was to keep the
world informed of news events in his part of the far North. He
was a local hero because of his efforts during a 1931 flu epidemic
at Barrow. Even though Morgan and his family contracted the disease, he stayed on duty, with a high fever, to use his radio to find

One of the first photographs taken of the crashed plane shortly after the bodies of Wiley and Will Rogers were removed in the early morning hours of August 16, 1935. The plane cast "an eerie shadow" in the semi-darkness of the Alaskan summer night near the top of the world. Courtesy Oklahoma Historical Society.

someone to bring medicine. Finally help came by way of airplane and dogsled. Morgan's rescue team had no idea who could have crashed 15 miles south of Barrow. Barrow was anticipating the arrival of Wiley and Will sometime in the next few days, but no one expected them from the southwest. Wiley would be flying from Fairbanks, from the southeast. That was the route Joe Crosson always took, and Crosson was surely advising Wiley on the flight.

During the trip to Okpeaha's camp, Sergeant Morgan asked Okpeaha for more details. It was only when Okpeaha described the plane's occupants as "one man with rag on sore eye and big man with boots" that Morgan and Daugherty figured out it could be Wiley and Will. It took Morgan and the rescue team nearly three hours to reach the crash scene.

Dense fog and the semi-darkness gave the upturned plane "a most ghostly appearance" Morgan later wrote, "Our hearts chilled at the thought of what we might find there... As we approached nearer the plane we soon realized no human could possibly survive the terrific crash. the plane was but a huge mass of twisted and broken wood and metal."[249]

The plane was "bottom up," its right wing broken, and the engine was deeply imbedded in water and sand. It had landed in three feet of clear water, within a large lagoon, not 100 yards from the sea, "a pretty place, a kindly landing place." Everything in the plane was broken, Will's typewriter, with an unfinished column in it, was twisted out of shape. Fishing rods and rifles were utterly destroyed.

Sergeant Morgan discovered that the natives had used axes to cut into the plane's cabin and recovered Will's body, but could not reach Wiley's corpse that was pinned against his seat by the engine. The plane had to be torn apart to free Wiley's body. Both bodies were carefully laid in sleeping bags found in the wreck and placed in the bottom of a small boat. Morgan reported how deeply the natives felt the loss of Wiley and Will. "As we started our slow trip back to Barrow one of the Eskimo boys began to sing a hymn in Eskimo and soon all the voices joined in this singing and continued until our arrival at Barrow when we silently bore the bodies from the beach to the hospital."[250]

Dr. Henry Greist and his wife Mollie operated a small hospital at Barrow that provided primitive medical treatment for the natives in the area. He was the only doctor for a thousand miles and also pastored three small Presbyterian congregations.

Dr. Greist recorded the injuries, "Both had suffered numerous fractures. . . Mr. Post had suffered a fearful abdominal wound, lacerations of the trunk and face. Mr. Rogers face was torn sadly, his

The pieces of the Orion-Explorer were hauled on a small barge back to Point Barrow. After the control panel and few other important parts were removed, Mae Post ordered the remainder of the plane to be destroyed. Mae unsuccessfully tried to fly to Point Barrow to see where her husband had died, but was turned back by bad weather. Courtesy *The Daily Oklahoman.*

scalp also torn from the skull in part, and he also had suffered a fracture of the frontal bone over the nasal region. . . It proved impossible to determine whether the two victims died instantly from their fearful injuries, or from drowning. . . Certain it is that both men lost consciousness instantly with the accident and suffered no pain, that death was sure and certain and quickly had."[251]

Mae Post was visiting friends in Ponca City, Oklahoma, when she received the tragic news. She broke down and told the wife of "Red" Gray, "I wish to God I had been with him when he crashed." Mae had just returned to Oklahoma from Seattle where she had made the decision not to go on the trip with Wiley and Will. The *New York Times* story said, "Prostrated by grief, Mrs. Post went to bed for several hours."[252]

Wiley's parents still did not have a telephone, and the radio they often used to follow the travels of their son was broken. Maysville Mayor Fred Scott and local newspaper publisher William Showen drove out to the farm with the sad news. Mrs. Post said, "This is the news we've been dreading for years." As word of Wiley's death spread throughout the farms around Maysville, neighbors and friends dropped what they were doing and hurried to the Post farm to offer their sympathy.

Betty Rogers was with her daughter Mary in Skowhegan, Maine, when she was told of her husband's death. She immediately returned to California to make funeral arrangements.

Within hours of the deaths of Wiley and Will, their old friend Colonel Charles Lindbergh took control of the massive project to get their bodies home to their loved ones. Lindbergh, in Maine to celebrate his son's birthday, cabled Dr. Greist at Barrow, saying he was acting as agent for the widows and that no one should move the bodies unless, he, Lindbergh, gave permission.

Lindbergh was a technical consultant to Pan American Airways and used his influence with the airline to devise a plan to fly the bodies home. Pacific Alaska Airways (PAA) was a subsidiary of Pan American. The job to fly to Barrow to pick up the bodies fell on none other than Joe Crosson, Wiley's friend and hunting companion, who was PAA's chief pilot.

This Associated Press Wirephoto was printed in the nation's newspapers, tracing the Alaska trip and the fatal crash. Courtesy *The Daily Oklahoman.*

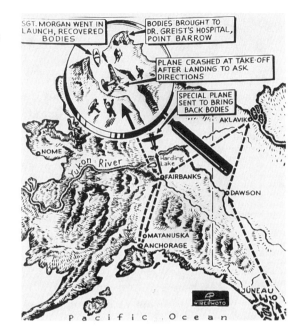

Crosson was legendary as a bush pilot in Alaska. After a stint as a pilot in World War I, he left California and found his home in Alaska, where he became known as the "mercy flier," for his many heroic trips to rescue stranded trappers and to deliver food to snowed-in outposts. His most famous flight had been to take serum to fight the influenza epidemic at Barrow in 1931. He battled blizzards, heavy winds, and 20-below-zero conditions to land with the serum at Barrow. It was so cold that it took him two hours to warm up his engines, but the settlement was saved.

Pan American president Juan T. Trippe offered whatever help was possible to the widows, "Although this is the saddest of missions, we are glad to be of service to the families of those two outstanding Americans who have done so much for aviation."[253]

The federal government announced its readiness to assist in getting the bodies of Wiley and Will home. The Treasury Department ordered the Coast Guard cutter Northland to sail to Barrow to lend any assistance needed.

No one knew northern Alaska better than Joe Crosson. He and

PAA's chief radio man, Robert Gleason, took off from Fairbanks in a seaplane that could land safely at Barrow. They arrived at Barrow, rested a few hours, and then loaded the bodies on the seaplane for the dangerous trip through fog and rain back to Fairbanks. The Associated Press reported:

> Through the same murky Arctic skies which lured them to death, the bodies of Will Rogers and Wiley Post were borne to Fairbanks today in the first phase of the long journey home. Joe Crosson, ace pilot of the Far North and close friend of the two men, made the dangerous 500-mile flight from Point Barrow in four and one-half hours.[254]

Thousands gathered at the Fairbanks dock on the Chena River as Crosson's pontooned airplane landed, almost at the same spot where Wiley and Will had taken off from less than two days before. The linen-wrapped bodies were unloaded from the plane and taken to a local funeral parlor for embalming.

The Canadian government gave Pan American Airways permission for Crosson to fly over Canada on the 2,000 mile trek from Fairbanks to Seattle. The bodies were loaded in a Pan American Lockheed 10 Electra and Crosson, tired from his ten-hour round trip to Barrow and back to Fairbanks, nosed the plane up into the frigid Arctic air.

Mae first planned to fly from Oklahoma to Seattle to meet the plane carrying her husband's body. Oil man Frank Phillips had placed his entire aviation department at her command. But at the last minute, Mae decide to stay with Mrs. "Red" Gray in Ponca City, who told the *New York Times,* "She is not strong enough to stand the trip, and she wants to be away from the crowds."[255]

On Sunday, Joe Crosson arrived in Seattle where he was greeted by 15,000 mourners. He had flown two days, so pilot William Winston, in a Pan American Douglas DC–2, took over the grim task of ferrying Will's body to his family in Los Angeles, and the winging toward Oklahoma City with the remains of Wiley. Joe Crosson could not stand the thought of leaving his dear friend, Wiley, and flew with Winston all the way to Oklahoma City.

The day after Wiley's and Will's death, both houses of the U.S. Congress paused to remember them, then unanimously passed legislation authorizing the Smithsonian Institution to pay up to $25,000 for the *Winnie Mae* and all of its original equipment.

It was fate that the bill was already scheduled on the Senate calendar for August 16. Oklahoma U. S. Senator Elmer Thomas spoke briefly before the bill was passed, "This is a fitting tribute to the brave explorer and intrepid pilot, Wiley Post, who went to his death today." Oklahoma's other U. S. Senator, Thomas Gore, said, "Today my state has suffered a double tragedy." Senate majority leader Joseph Robinson called Wiley, "a courageous representative of a gallant group who, on wings of adventure, sought remote places and conquered long distances."[256]

President Franklin Roosevelt expressed the nation's official grief and cited Wiley for "leaving behind a splendid contribution to the science of aviation." Former president Herbert Hoover called Wiley and Will "great souls" and said he felt a deep personal loss in their passing.

On August 16, just 24 hours after the crash, NBC broadcast a stirring tribute to the memory of Wiley and Will. The coast-to-coast, live broadcast featured tributes from Vice President Charles Curtis, Congressmen Jed Johnson and Josh Lee of Oklahoma, House Speaker Joseph T. Byrnes, Senate Democratic leader Joseph T. Robinson, Senator Thomas Gore of Oklahoma, former Secretary of War Patrick Hurley, and several of Hollywood's leading actors and movie company owners.

From all over the globe, in dozens of languages, came tributes to Wiley and Will. New York City Mayor F. H. La Guardia called the loss, "not only a national one; it will be felt throughout the world. We have lost a great and courageous flier, another martyr to the progress of aviation development." Former New York Governor Alfred E. Smith said the two great Americans would be missed by everybody. Actress Mary Pickford said Will and Wiley "gave gloriously of every moment, enriching our lives with the treasures of their accomplishments."

Brazil's leading newspaper, *O Globo,* said, "Two famous Americans' lives have been stolen." German war ace Ernst Udet told the Associated Press that he considered Wiley the "greatest flier of all time." French newspapers printed long biographies of Wiley and Will, as did newspapers in almost every city in the world. In Berlin, where Wiley had been long lauded as an aviation hero, the Tageblatt paid homage to Wiley by calling him a "brusque, rough adventurer, a solid flying fanatic."

Captain Eddie Rickenbacker, American World War I ace and general manager of Eastern Airlines, called both Wiley and Will aviation pioneers, and Will "not just a passenger, but a fellow adventurer." He called Wiley's death a serious blow to the science of flying. "The pioneer spirit is what set Post apart from the usual run of expert flyers. He saw what ought to be done. Then he found out how to do it. Then he went and did it."[257]

"When the news came," wrote the Oakland, California *Tribune,* "it was met with an all but determined will not to believe. It seemed incredible that two who were so light-hearted and friendly, so secure in popular regard, could have departed so suddenly."[258]

The *Detroit Free Press* called the crash that killed Wiley and Will "a sad public misfortune." Amelia Earhart called Wiley "the bravest of the brave, . . . In addition to his willingness to share with others anything he had found out about planes or motors, his most dominant characteristic was his complete unconsciousness that what he did had any value or color. So close was he to his profession that he could not see the sheen on his own wings."[259]

Kings and queens and leaders from every continent sent telegrams of condolence to Mae and Betty. The outpouring of the world's grief was genuine. But the loss was greatest in Oklahoma who had lost its famous citizens. Governor E. W. Marland said, "The state will want to give them a memorial, but the state can't add anything to the honors already heaped upon them by the sovereigns and people of the world."

Flags in Oklahoma were ordered to half-staff. A black crepe bow was tied to the propeller of the *Winnie Mae* in a hangar in Bartlesville. Oklahoma mourned deeply. Photographs of Wiley and Will, "draped in crepe," were placed in many shop windows.

Children hung flowers under the name plate of Wiley Post Playground in Oklahoma City, while the Wiley Post Air Corps had the air sleeve on tops of its hangar dyed black.[260]

The Daily Oklahoman, in an August 17 editorial eloquently described Oklahoma's loss:

> Death is doubly cruel in depriving Oklahoma of her two outstanding citizens... Both of the men who have gone from Oklahoma prairies to win world fame have died in a single day. Only one swing of the scythe of death, and the two best known of all Oklahomans have gone beyond the stars.
>
> Words are futile, inadequate, helpless things in all real crises... All the wealth of all vocabularies might be employed, but in this hour of Oklahoma's bereavement words of grief and words of praise are nothing more important than the crying of an infant in the night. Perhaps utter silence would be the most fitting tribute that a stricken people could pay to Will Rogers and Wiley Post...
>
> The tragedy that darted down from Arctic clouds claimed men who had entrenched themselves in the love and admiration of a world. But this universal sorrow is climaxed in Oklahoma. It is most bitter on the old Cherokee prairies where the people remember Will Rogers as a boy. It is supremely bitter in the fields of broomcorn and among the derricks where Wiley Post first caught the eagle's spirit and resolved to cross clouds and sky...
>
> There is nothing Oklahoma can do to add one whit to the fame these men have achieved. One has made his name familiar wherever English words are spoken. The other has set a mark for all future aviators, for no greater birdman has ever defied and conquered skies and seas. Let funeral dirges and the anthems of sorrow attest the grief of Oklahomans, but the achievements of Will Rogers and Wiley Post have builded monuments more durable than bronze.[261]

A FINAL RESTING PLACE

Over the route he followed in triumph at the end of his world
flight, Wiley Post flew home Tuesday. At the municipal airport a
crowd of spectators lined the fence, friends waited in the shade.
Wiley made a beautiful three-point landing. The ship stopped, but
there were bowed heads instead of cheers. The tragic difference in
Tuesday's scene from the setting of bygone days was—Wiley Post was
dead.[262]

ITH THOSE WORDS *The Daily Oklahoman* began its August 21 story of the return of Wiley's body from Alaska, a four-day flight, surely the longest funeral flight in history. Eight thousand people lined the runway at Oklahoma City's Municipal Airport to pay silent tribute to their fallen hero as the Pan American plane taxied with Wiley for the last time over "the black runways that hold his footprints in their soft surface."

Police officers saluted, men removed their hats and women bowed their heads as the plane moved toward an open hangar. The ship entered the cleared hangar under its own power and the doors were closed "before the glistening propellers stopped." Behind the doors the broken body of the only man to fly around the world alone was "given from the hands of those who brought it so carefully to friends at home."[263]

With a motorcycle police escort, a hearse carried Wiley's body to the Watts and McAtee Funeral Home where "those who wish to view the body" could do so from 8:00 to 10:00 A.M. on Wednesday, August 21. Thousands paraded by Wiley's casket at the funeral home, which extended the viewing time until 11:00 A.M., the appointed time for the historic funeral cortege to leave Oklahoma City for the solemn trip to Maysville, 60 miles away.

Two Oklahoma Highway Patrol cars led the funeral procession south on Highway 77, followed by the hearse and an automobile occupied by oil man Frank Phillips, pilot Billy Parker, and Joe Crosson, who had brought Wiley's body home to Oklahoma. Residents of every town and community lined the highway. A newspaper reported, "The muffled police siren moaned like the low roll of funeral drums. Especially at Purcell was there a tremendous tribute paid the renowned flier. Thousands stood at the curb, reverently removing their hats. The curbs were lined with flags at half-mast."[264] The procession left a trail of dust as it approached Maysville. Ten national guardsmen, from Company C of the 120th Engineers in Norman, stood with bayoneted rifles and formed a lane through which the coffin was carried into the Landmark Missionary Baptist Church. A young reporter observed, "As if all nature was joining in the tribute to Oklahoma's hero, murmured cannonades of thunder came from a bank of low-lying clouds in the south, trees stirred in a cool north breeze, and the skies were dabbled white and gray."[265]

More than seven thousand people stood under the trees and in the tall grass around the little white church for hours, dressed in their Sunday best, or shirt sleeves, or overalls. Wiley Post was, in real life, a common man, and rich and poor alike came to his funeral. There were farmers from the cotton field, barefoot boys and girls, housewives, merchants and filling station attendants.

Newsreel cameras and still photographers recorded for history the scene of "homely grieving." Local newspaper editor W. E. Showen introduced Oklahoma Attorney General Mac Q. Williamson who addressed the waiting throng:

A good many years ago one of our good citizens transferred his family from Texas to the Washita Valley. That was the family of Wiley Post. Even then Wiley was fired with ambition to do something for his family, for aviation, and for himself, with no more than the opportunity of the average boy in the average county. Not content with everyday existence, Wiley went on to the far reaches of the air, making his name second to none in his chosen calling. My friends, a lovable, noble, courageous soul has found rest and peace.[266]

Most of the seats had been removed from the church so the thousands who had gathered could walk, two by two, through the church. It took more than two hours for the mourners to move from their location under the maple and sycamore trees into the one-room church, past the coffin, and out the back door.

Sheriffs deputies and city police officers for miles around had been brought in for traffic and crowd control, but they were not needed. A newspaper story commented, "For these were not morbidly curious strangers, but the friends who watched Post as a fledgling and read about him as an eagle. They moved slowly and sorrowfully, cooling themselves with waving fans, as locusts sang a dirge in the trees."[267]

J. I. Dendy, principal of the Whitehead elementary school near Maysville, brought 140 children with him for the occasion. He said he wanted his students, mostly the children of cotton farmers, to see one boy who "left the cotton patch and made something of himself." Dendy wanted his students to realize they might do the same.

Late in the afternoon, the church was emptied to make ready for the Post family. Wiley's parents, wife, and brothers and sister rode in a caravan of seven cars to the door of the church. Several thousand people stood silent and respectful as the family went inside. It was the first time that the family members had seen Wiley's face since he left on his perilous journey to Alaska.

The "lamentations and cries of the women folk" reached the quiet, sorrowful friends outside. Mrs. W. F. Post, Wiley's white-haired mother, left the church aided by two national guard officers. "My darling's gone. My darling boy is gone," she cried. Wiley's father also had to be assisted, Mae Post, the widow, "collapsed as she was placed in the automobile."[268]

Wiley's parents pose with a picture of their dead son. Courtesy *The Daily Oklahoman*.

After the family left, the church was reopened for another 1,000 people who had come to view Wiley's body.

When Maysville newspaper editor Showen saw Wiley's body, he thought he saw the dead pilot move, "Of course it was imagination, for the immortal part of Wiley was at that moment piloting a phantom spirit ship in the ethereal realm, where there are no treacherous air pockets, no fogs, and mists and sudden storms to wreck his ship and force a perilous landing."[269]

Joe Crosson sat on the front porch of the Post home near Maysville as Wiley's parents tried some way to thank him for bringing their son's body home. Mrs. Post could only say, "Thank you my boy, and may God bless you and protect you." Crosson, standing between Mr. and Mrs. Post, holding their hands, had received his reward, the "kind that only a broken-hearted mother and father can give."[270]

Crosson spent a few minutes consoling Mae Post, as she sat alone in a nearby car, and then returned to the church for the procession back to Oklahoma City.

The Associated Press sent a reporter to downtown Maysville that night to hear the common folk talk about their dead hero. As in many small towns, Saturday night was the biggest night of the week in Maysville, with farmers completing their chores and coming to town just to sit and talk on Main Street. Fred Berry pointed to the corner of an auto dealer's office and said, "He sat right here and told me all the details of his last world flight." Another Maysville resident said, "Wiley was never talkative. He'd just stand around the streets or up against a tree, grinning, and talk like one of the boys. He never forgot his people."

President Roosevelt declared Thursday a National Day of Mourning, and ordered flags lowered to half-mast in honor of Wiley and Will. *The Daily Oklahoman* headline read: WHOLE WORLD TO JOIN CITY IN TRIBUTE TO POST TODAY

Will Rogers' funeral was scheduled in California for the same day. The *Oklahoman* lead editorial, entitled "Journey's End," tried to express the grief felt by the state:

> It is the melancholy duty of Oklahomans to mourn on a single day the passing of one who has been called the most popular man that ever lived and another one who has been called by competent authorities the greatest flier of all time. Oklahoma's cup of grief would be bitterly full if only one of her gifted sons were receiving his burial rites today. But both of those who won world renown in separate fields of adventure are sinking simultaneously into earth's everlasting embrace. Nothing is spared Oklahomans today. Nothing can mute the sorrow of Oklahomans as they view the march of their state's immortals into eternal rest. . . There is but one heart in Oklahoma and that heart is unutterably sore.[271]

In near 100-degree temperatures, 20,000 people gathered on the south steps of the State Capitol building to pass by Wiley's casket that lay in state in the capitol rotunda from 10 A.M. to noon. Less than half of the throng was able to get inside the capitol building. The newspaper account was graphic:

Above: Wiley's body lay in state in the rotunda of the Oklahoma State Capitol building for two hours on the day of his funeral.

Right: An honor guard carried Wiley's casket from the State Capitol rotunda to a waiting hearse. Twenty thousand people waited outside the building in 97-degree heat to honor their fallen hero. Courtesy *The Daily Oklahoman.*

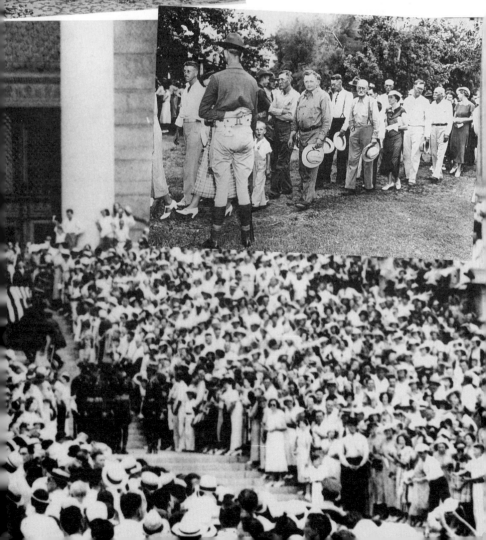

Left: At the one-room Landmark Missionary Baptist Church in Maysville, Wiley's casket was guarded by Oklahoma national guardsmen Private H.W. Mertes, Prague (left), and Corporal E.W. Ward, Lexington. Courtesy *The Daily Oklahoman.*

Below: Seven thousand mourners stood in line outside the church in Maysville.

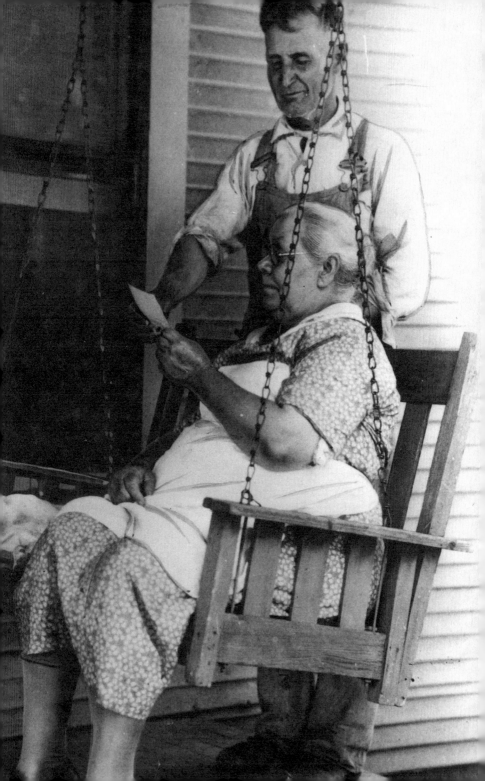

As steaming bodies jammed into close-packed lines, air became stifling, breathing was difficult. All windows and doors in the capitol were thrown open, but it brought little relief. Women and children fainted and men carried them outside. Others surged inward to take their places. National guardsmen in sweat-soaked uniforms worked feverishly to keep the unwieldy mass under control. Ropes were strung along the rotunda to keep lines from breaking. Old and young were represented, barefooted boys scurried through halls, all conscious of playing a part in a moment of Oklahoma history. Two aged women, tottering and exhausted, gazed hopelessly at the long line ahead. 'We knew Wiley personally,' one said to a guardsman.[272]

Governor Marland strode to the rotunda flanked by Ft. Sill commander Brigadier General H.W. Butner, President Roosevelt's personal envoy to the funeral. Marland stood by Wiley's bronze and copper casket and spoke in hushed tones:

> Wiley Post has come here to rest. Nothing we poor mortals can say or do will add to the lasting glory of prestige of Oklahoma's son. Wiley Post flew around the earth. He ascended above the earth to heights unattained by man. Today he precedes us, his friends, on that greater journey we all must take some day... Happy landing Wiley Post in that heaven of all brave souls... Happy landing.[273]

As eight national guardsmen carried the casket down the capitol steps at noon, airplanes flew low over the capitol, dropping flowers to the sea of people below. A motorcycle escort took the casket to the First Baptist Church in downtown Oklahoma City.

Frank Phillips was the chairman of 150 honorary pall-bearers that included Oklahoma's two U.S. Senators, Thomas Gore and Elmer Thomas, Governor Marland, former governor Lee Cruce, Harold Gatty, Walter Beech, famous aircraft manufacturer, U.S.

Mr. and Mrs. W.F. Post on the front porch of their modest Maysville farm home, reading condolences from Wiley's fans. Courtesy *The Daily Oklahoman.*

Secretary of State Cordell Hull, Paul Braniff, and Walter Harrison. The eight active pall-bearers who bore the casket into the church were Leslie Fain, Harry G. Frederickson, Joe Crosson, Bennie Turner, Ted Colbert, Wiley's friend from Ponca City, Billy Parker, Ernest Shults, and "Red" Gray.

The greats in American aviation gathered to honor Wiley. Amelia Earhart sat with transatlantic fliers Bennett Griffin and Jimmy Mattern, and record-setting pilot Art Goebel.

It seemed that the whole world sent flowers to the funeral. Massive tiers of flowers graced the front of the sanctuary of the First Baptist Church. The Soviet ambassador to the United States, A.A. Troyanovsky, sent a wreath of 500 carnations. From Betty Rogers came a great blanket of gardenias. Frank Phillips sent a large American flag floral arrangement of red, white, and blue

Flowers for Wiley's funeral jammed the front of the First Baptist Church in downtown Oklahoma City, August 23, 1935. Note the sections of the church reserved for "state officials," "city officials," and "active pallbearers."

Nearly 20,000 people waited outside the church as the two ministers lead the procession of the casket and family down the steps to the hearse. Courtesy Oklahoma Historical Society.

gladiolas. Mr. and Mrs. Joe Crosson expressed their sympathy with a large propeller made from flowers, and the Wiley Post Aircraft Company sent a floral replica of the *Winnie Mae*. Other flowers from governors, congressmen, and world leaders were literally stacked at the front of the church. After the funeral Mae Post ordered the flowers distributed to Oklahoma City hospitals.

The 2:00 P.M. service was conducted by First Baptist pastor Reverend William Richardson "Billy" White and Reverend J. H. Gardner of Sentinel, Oklahoma. Reverend Gardner was once Wiley's Sunday school teacher. The church seated 2,000 people and was packed to the rafters. Thousands unable to get inside waited on the streets to catch a glimpse of the family and Joe Crosson who had himself been made a hero by the American press. A public address system allowed the large crowd on the streets to hear the service.

It was the largest funeral in the history of Oklahoma. Some reporters estimated as many as 40,000 people were within a two-block radius of the First Baptist Church. Funeral director Tipp Watts of the Watts and McAtee funeral home estimated that 75,000 people either attended the funeral or paid tribute to Wiley along the funeral route from the State Capitol to the First Baptist Church. The church used two and a half tons of ice to cool the building for the funeral.

The service was carried live on radio stations KOMA and WKY in Oklahoma City. Police chief John Watt directed his officers in blocking off several streets around the church to make it easier for family and close friends to park.

In only a few years, Reverend White had turned First Baptist Church of Oklahoma City into the second largest congregation in the Southern Baptist Convention. He was a kind, humble man who was known as a master orator. He later served as president of Hardin-Simmons University and Baylor University. He mesmerized the audience at Wiley's funeral, saying, "He died doing what he wanted to do. Flying was his supreme emotion and passion. It was in flying that Wiley Post found himself. It was in this endeavor that he lived, moved and had his being."[274]

Reverend White took his text from Isaiah 60:8: "Who are these that fly as a cloud, and as the doves to their windows?" In his brief sermon, he expressed the hope that "He and his pal soared beyond the stratosphere, and that some day sorrowing ones left behind will be called up to meet them in the air, to be forever with the Lord."

Reverend Evans, the pastor of the Landmark Missionary Baptist Church in Maysville, said, "Upon the wings of faith, the soul of Wiley Post has taken flight to soar to greater heights than ever it knew here below."[275]

The large crowd filed out of the church as the organ played the old hymn "In The Sweet Bye and Bye." Only the Post family remained. The casket had been closed since it lay in state at the State Capitol, but was reopened for the family.

The hearse was followed by hundreds of cars as it headed up

North Robinson Street toward the Fairlawn Cemetery mausoleum where Wiley's body would stay overnight until Mae decidedly exactly where he would be buried. The U. S. Congress had approved a resolution allowing the American hero to be buried in Arlington National Cemetery across the Potomac River from the nation's capital. Wiley's father wanted his son buried at Maysville. In the end, Mae picked Memorial Park Cemetery in far north Oklahoma City as Wiley's final resting place.

The procession to Fairlawn Cemetery after the funeral was a somber drive. As the hearse passed the fire station near N.W. 23rd and Western, firefighters stood at rigid attention beside their red fire trucks. Literally thousands of automobiles lined the street ahead of the procession.

Ten thousand more people waited at the cemetery. The hearse stopped at the steps of the mausoleum, and the flag-draped casket was carried up the white limestone steps into the dimly lighted chapel. After Reverend Gardner said a few words of encouragement to the family, taps sounded, and the doors closed as the family left the building.

As Wiley was being eulogized at his funeral in Oklahoma City, aviators all over the nation paid homage to their friend. In New York, more than a million people watched a group of 24 planes fly from Floyd Bennett Field on Long Island, up the Hudson River, and across Manhattan and Brooklyn.

Airplanes flew over a large memorial service in Philadelphia. Ten thousand visitors at the Pacific International Exposition in San Diego, California, paused to hear taps played to honor Wiley and Will. In far away Alaska, all 22 U. S. Signal Corps radio stations observed five minutes of silence at high noon.

The Daily Oklahoman summed up the day:

Wiley Post flew solo Thursday night. After the most reverent and highest tribute the nation and state could pay, Wiley Post was as he conquered the world from the air—alone.[276]

THE YEARS SINCE

Wiley Post's flight remains the most remarkable flight in
history—

HOWARD HUGHES

THERE WAS MUCH finger-pointing during the investigation into the cause of the crash that killed Wiley and Will. Newspapers said Joe Crosson had advised Wiley not to fly that day, a charge that Crosson vehemently denied. The Bureau of Air Commerce was blamed for not inspecting the Orion-Explorer for air worthiness after the pontoons were added in Seattle. In the end, the official report did not find fault with Wiley. It was the opinion of the accident board that the probable cause of this accident was "loss of control of the aircraft at a low altitude, after sudden engine failure, due to the extreme nose-heaviness of the aircraft."[277]

Facing page: The final resting place for Wiley Post was this plot in Memorial Park Cemetery in far north Oklahoma City. Mae was buried beside Wiley when she died almost a half-century later in 1984. Courtesy *The Daily Oklahoman.*

The engine had been buried in mud and 1935 technology would not allow the cause of the engine failure to be determined. The engine was still warm when Wiley re-started it after asking directions from Clair Okpeaha. One expert theorized that carburetor icing may have caused the engine to quit. The crash occurred because, once the engine failed, Wiley could not control the plane adequately to glide to a landing. The addition of the pontoons and the plane's nose-heaviness and the low altitude culminated in Wiley's inability to pull out of the stall.

Mae sold the *Winnie Mae* to the Smithsonian Institution for $25,000. Paul Garber and Billy Parker oversaw the dismantling of the airplane in Bartlesville and loaded the pieces onto a railroad car for the trip to Washington, D.C. The *Winnie Mae* was put back together and displayed by December, 1935. Wiley's plane and his pressurized flying suit are still prominently displayed in the National Air and Space Museum. Mae used the money from the sale of the *Winnie Mae* to buy a farm in Ralls, near Lubbock, in the Texas Panhandle. She lived a peaceful life, never remarried, and was buried beside her husband at Memorial Park Cemetery in Oklahoma City when she died in 1984.

The month after Wiley's death a bronze plaque was installed at Floyd Bennett Field in Brooklyn, commemorating the spot where Wiley landed after his 1933 flight around the world.

In December, 1936, Wiley was posthumously honored when Mae was presented with the gold medal of the Federation Aeronautique Internationale, the highest award in aviation. Frank Phillips chaired a committee that arranged a very special banquet in Tulsa. Aviation pioneers Amon Carter, Eddie Rickenbacker, Frank Hawks, Art Goebel, Jimmy Doolittle, Jimmy Mattern, and Joe Crosson were guests of honor. Phillips said the greatest memorial to Wiley was aviation itself, "The luxurious air transports that

Mae sold the *Winnie Mae* for display in the Smithsonian Institution. The plane was on permanent display within four months of Wiley's death in August, 1935. Courtesy Oklahoma Historical Society.

soar from coast to coast in 14 hours, the clipper ships which fly the ocean, every landing field, every winking beacon, are all in the finest sense a tribute and memorial to Wiley Post." *The Daily Oklahoman* lauded the world of aviation for honoring Wiley, "Were Post still here, he'd grin, shuffle his feet, stuff the medal in his pocket and talk about other things. No pilot can receive the world's highest distinction without high pride. Wiley would be no exception, but Wiley would want no blare of trumpets."

Many honors were bestowed upon Wiley after his death. The rotating beacon on the George Washington Bridge in New York City was named the Will Rogers-Wiley Post Beacon. The airport observation deck at the Newark, New Jersey airport was named after Wiley and Will. Wiley was awarded the Distinguished Flying Cross by the U.S. Congress.

Shortly after the crash a monument was erected near the sight in Alaska where Wiley and Will died. In 1982 the Oklahoma Air National Guard flew a delegation of Oklahomans to Point Barrow for the dedication of a new granite monument across the street from the Wiley Post–Will Rogers Airport at Barrow. State Representative Stratton Taylor of Claremore and Will Rogers Memorial

Curator Dr. Reba Collins led the delegation at the unveiling of the $50,000 memorial. The Lions Clubs of Claremore, Oklahoma and Barrow, Alaska co-sponsored the project. The star of the August 16, 1982 dedication was James Rogers, the second son of Will Rogers, who was "the spitting image of Will himself."

A privately-owned airport near North May and Britton Road in Oklahoma City was named Wiley Post Field shortly after Wiley's death. In 1961, Tulakes Airport, Oklahoma City's primary general aviation airport, was renamed Wiley Post Airport. On October 22, during dedication ceremonies attended by 1,500 people, Mae removed a blue satin veil from a bust of Wiley sculpted by Leonard McMurray. Mae said, "I want to cry but I can't do it here." The bronze bust still stands in the entrance hall of the airport administration building. On the wall beside the bust is a large photograph of Wiley standing in front of his beloved *Winnie Mae*.

Before the dedication of Wiley Post Airport, Reverend. W. R. White, who had officiated at Wiley's funeral 26 years before, spoke at a brief memorial service at Memorial Park Cemetery. General

The Oklahoma Historical Society Building was built in 1929 and renamed for Wiley Post in the early 1950's. The building houses the state's historical museum, the control panel of the ill-fated Orion-Explorer, and busts of Wiley and Will Rogers, presented to the Historical Society by oil man Frank Phillips in 1937. Courtesy Oklahoma Historical Society.

Maurice Marrs, Wiley Post Airport supervisor, circled the cemetery in an Aero Commander dropping flowers reminiscent of those showered from planes on the day of Wiley's funeral in 1935.

U. S. Senator Mike Monroney of Oklahoma paid tribute to Wiley in a 1961 speech on the floor of the U.S. Senate:

> It has always seemed to me that Wiley Post has never been given the recognition he deserved. Primitive and homemade though his equipment was, he met and conquered many of the problems involved in high altitude flight. . . He foresaw, and helped to create, many of the miracles of aviation which we enjoy today.[278]

On September 26, 1963, the Oklahoma City Chamber of Commerce dedicated a statute of Wiley by Leonard McMurry, in the Civic Center in downtown Oklahoma City. Tulakes Airport, Oklahoma City's primary general aviation airport, was renamed Wiley Post Airport in 1961. At left is the modern control tower and administration building.

The U.S. Postal Service issued two airmail stamps in 1969 commemorating Wiley's achievements in flight. Mae looks at oversized replicas of the stamps in first-day-of-issue ceremonies in Oklahoma City. Courtesy Oklahoma Historical Society,

The original memorial built overlooking the area where Wiley and Will Rogers crashed at Point Barrow, Alaska. In 1982 Oklahoma State Representative Stratton Taylor of Claremore and Will Rogers Memorial Curator Dr. Reba Collins led a delegation to Point Barrow to dedicate a new monument. Courtesy Oklahoma Historical Society.

Oklahoma City civic leader Sylvan N. Goldman provided this bronze bust of Wiley that is displayed in the lobby of the administration building of Wiley Post Airport in Oklahoma City.

The Oklahoma Historical Society museum just southeast of the State Capitol building in Oklahoma City was renamed the Wiley Post Memorial Building. Even today, one can see a display of the original telegrams sent to Mae following Wiley's death, the instrument panel from the Orion-Explorer that crashed near Point Barrow, and Wiley's watch that stopped at 8:18 on August 15, 1935. A bronze bust of Wiley, a gift of Frank Phillips to the people of Oklahoma, eternally watches over the ornate hallway on the first floor of the Wiley Post Building.

In 1963 a larger-than-life statue of Wiley standing by a globe was unveiled in the park between Oklahoma City's Civic Center Music Hall and the Municipal Building. Just east of Wiley's statue now stands a statue of Oklahoma astronaut Thomas P. Stafford, a modern pioneer in America's space program.

Mae Post (left) and Wiley's youngest brother, Gordon, view a new portrait of Wiley unveiled at the Oklahoma Historical Society in 1980. Courtesy Oklahoma Historical Society.

The U. S. Postal Service issued two airmail stamps honoring Wiley in 1979. A special first-day-of-issue ceremony was held on November 20 at the Wiley Post Memorial Building. Guests included Mae, Wiley's brother, Gordon, and his sister, Mary.

A new high school in Maysville was built two years after Wiley died and named after the deceased flier. Today the Wiley Post Elementary School is part of the Putnam City School District in far northwest Oklahoma City.

In July, 1938, Howard Hughes flew around the world in three days and 19 hours. Hughes flew a twin-engine Lockheed, technically far advanced of the *Winnie Mae*. When Hughes was asked to compare his flight with Wiley's 1933 flight, he told reporters:

> Wiley Post's flight remains the most remarkable flight in history. It can never be duplicated. He did it alone! To make a trip of that kind is beyond comprehension. It's like pulling a rabbit out of a hat or sawing a woman in half.[279]

It has been more than six decades since Wiley Post flew alone around the earth. For the rest of time, whenever aviation buffs gather to sip coffee and talk about the magnetic topic of flying, Wiley's personal achievement of soloing around the world in the plywood contraption known as the *Winnie Mae* will be called the most unique flight in all aviation history.

His pressurized flying suit was the forerunner of the modern space suit. His discoveries paved the way for man to visit the moon. . . and beyond. Whenever you see an astronaut walking in space, safe within a pressurized suit, think of Wiley. The next time you ride in a jetliner cruising along at ease at 35,000 feet, think of Wiley and his *Winnie Mae* climbing into the stratosphere over Bartlesville.

As man strives to build even better spaceships to reach farther into the universe, every advance will carry a bit of Wiley's dream. In terms of human endurance and achievement, Wiley Post was the world's greatest pilot, for all time.

1. Stanley R. Mohler and Bobby Johnson, *Wiley Post, His Winnie Mae, and the World's First Pressure Suit* (Washington, D.C.: Smithsonian Institution Press, 1971), 85-88.

2. *New York Times,* August 17, 1935.

3. Mohler, Wiley Post, 86.

4. *Wiley Post and Harold Gatty, Around the World in Eight Days* (New York: Garden City Publishing Company, 1931), 240.

5. Ibid., 241.

6. Ibid., 242.

7. Ibid., 243.

8. Ibid., 244.

9. Ibid., 245.

10. Ibid., 246.

11. Ibid., 247.

12. Ibid., 248.

13. Mohler, *Wiley Post,* 1.

14. Post, *Eight Days,* 250.

15. Odie B. Faulk, *Jennys to Jets,* (Muskogee, Oklahoma: Western Heritage Books Inc., 1983), 79.

16. Post, *Eight Days,* 251

17. *Chickasha Star,* April 2, 1921.

18. Information taken from the police blotter of the Grady County Sheriff's Office, vertical file of the Oklahoma Historical Society.

19. Parole agreement between Wiley and the Oklahoma Department of Corrections, vertical file of the Oklahoma Historical Society.

20. Ibid.

21. Post, *Eight Days,* 251.

22. Louise Welsh, Willa Mae Townes, John Morris, *A History of the Greater Seminole Oil Field* (Oklahoma City: Western Heritage Books, 1981), dust jacket.

23. Mohler, *Wiley Post,* 3.

24. Post, *Eight Days,* 254-255.

25. Ibid., 256.

26. Ibid., 257.

27. Ibid., 258.

28. Ibid., 259.

29. Mohler, *Wiley Post,* 4.

30. Post, *Eight Days,* 265.

31. Ibid., 263.

32. Ibid., 260.

33. Mohler, *Wiley Post,* 4.

34. Ibid.

35. Post, *Eight Days,* 265.

36. Faulk, *Jennys to Jets,* 118.

37. Post, *Eight Days,* 266.

38. January 28, 1956 interview with Arthur Oakley by Gary Hartsell, now held by the oral history department of the Oklahoma Historical Society.

39. Post, *Eight Days,* 267.

40. Ibid.

41. June 16, 1993 interview with Eula Pearl Scott by Bill Pitts, now held by the oral history department of the Oklahoma Historical Society.

42. Ibid.

43. Mohler, *Wiley Post,* 5.

44. Ibid., 6.

45. Ibid., 7.

46. Ibid.

47. Post, *Eight Days,* 270-271.

48. Ibid., 271.

49. Ibid., 273.

50. Ibid.

51. Bob Burke and Von Russell Creel, *Lyle Boren: Rebel Congressman* (Oklahoma City, Western Heritage Books, 1991), 31-32.

52. Post, *Eight Days,* 276.

53. Ibid., 277.

54. Ibid., 278.

55. Ibid., 13-14.

56. Ibid., 279-280.

57. Ibid., 280.

58. Ibid., 281.

59. Ibid., 19.

60. Ibid., 20.

61. Ibid., 21.

62. Ibid., 22.

63. Ibid., 23.

64. Ibid., 25.

65. Ibid., 26.

66. Mohler, *Wiley Post,* 19.

67. Post, *Eight Days,* 31.

68. Ibid., 37-38.

69. Ibid., 38.

70. Ibid., 53.

71. Mohler, *Wiley Post,* 20-21.

72. Ibid., 22.

73. Ibid.

74. Ibid.

75. Post, *Eight Days,* 57.

76. Ibid.

77. Ibid., 60.

78. Ibid., 58.

79. Ibid., 62.

80. Ibid., 65.

81. Ibid., 68.

82. Ibid., 69.

83. Ibid., 71.

84. *New York Times,* June 24, 1931.

85. Post, *Eight Days,* 71.

86. *New York Times,* June 24, 1931.

87. Post, *Eight Days,* 77.

88. *New York Times,* June 25, 1931.

89. Post, *Eight Days,* 85.

90. *New York Times,* June 25, 1931.

91. Post, *Eight Days,* 87.

92. Ibid., 91-92.

93. Ibid., 98.

94. Ibid., 101.

95. Ibid., 103-104.

96. Ibid., 109.

97. *New York Times,* June 25, 1931.

98. Post, *Eight Days,* 115.

99. Ibid., 121.

100. Ibid., 122.

101. *New York Times,* June 25, 1931.

102. Post, *Eight Days,* 123.

103. Ibid., 125.

104. *New York Times,* June 25, 1931.

105. Ibid.

106. Ibid.

107. Post, *Eight Days,* 130.

108. Ibid., 140.

109. Ibid., 141.

110. Ibid., 143.

111. Ibid., 145.

112. *New York Times,* June 26, 1931.

113. Post, *Eight Days,* 146.

114. Mohler, *Wiley Post,* 23.

115. Post, *Eight Days,* 148.

116. Ibid., 151.

117. Ibid., 152.

118. Ibid., 163.

119. Ibid., 164.

120. *New York Times,* June 27, 1931.

121. Post, *Eight Days,* 171.

122. Ibid., 172.

123. Ibid., 173

124. *New York Times,* June 28, 1931.

125. Post, *Eight Days,* 176.

126. *New York Times,* June 28, 1931.

127. Post, *Eight Days,* 179.

128. Ibid., 182.

129. Ibid., 183.

130. Ibid., 184.

131. Ibid., 187.

132. Ibid., 188.

133. Ibid., 197.

134. Ibid., 199.

135. Ibid., 201.

136. Ibid., 202.

137. Ibid., 205.

138. Ibid., 213.

139. Ibid., 214.

140. Ibid., 216.

141. *New York Times,* July 1, 1931.

142. Post, *Eight Days,* 216.

143. Ibid., 217.

144. Ibid., 218.

145. Ibid., 222.

146. Ibid., 224.

147. Ibid., 225.

148. *New York Times,* July 1, 1933.

149. Ibid.

150. Post, *Eight Days,* 229.

151. Ibid., 233

152. *New York Times,* July 2, 1931.

153. Ibid.

154. Ibid.

155. Ibid.

156. Ibid.

157. *New York Times,* July 4, 1931.

158. *The Daily Oklahoman,* July 5, 1931.

159. Ibid.

160. *New York Times,* July 2, 1931.

161. Post, *Eight Days,* 235.

162. *New York Times,* July 3, 1931.

163. Ibid.

164. Ibid.

165. Ibid.

166. Mohler, *Wiley Post,* 34.

167. Ibid.

168. *New York Times,* July 3, 1931.

169. Ibid.

170. Mohler, *Wiley Post,* 35.

171. Ibid.

172. Ibid. 36.

173. Ibid.

174. Analysis of Wiley Post prepared by Oklahoma City psychologist Dr. Stephen Carella. Dr. Carella reviewed all available information on Wiley's melancholic problem in prison and his mood swings as described by his friends. The analysis is contained in a letter from Dr. Carella to the author, May 31, 1996.

175. Ibid.

176. Ibid.

177. Mohler, *Wiley Post,* 39.

178. Ibid., 46-47.

179. Ibid., 40.

180. Ibid., 41.

181. Ibid.

182. Ibid., 43.

183. *New York Times,* May 28, 1933.

184. Mohler, *Wiley Post,* 44.

185. Faulk, *Jennys to Jets,* 152.

186. Mohler, *Wiley Post,* 44.

187. *The Daily Oklahoman,* June 30, 1933.

188. Mohler, *Wiley Post,* 51.

189. *The Daily Oklahoman,* June 27, 1933.

190. Mohler, *Wiley Post,* 55.

191. *New York Times,* July 15, 1933.

192. *New York Times,* July 16, 1933.

193. *The Daily Oklahoman,* August 15, 1982.

194. Mohler, *Wiley Post,* 58.

195. *New York Times,* July 18, 1933.

196. Ibid., July 17, 1933.

197. Ibid., July 18, 1933.

198. Ibid., July 17, 1933.

199. Ibid., July 18, 1933.

200. Ibid., July 19, 1933.

201. Mohler, *Wiley Post,* 62.

202. *New York Times,* July 19, 1933.

203. Mohler, *Wiley Post,* 64.

204. *New York Times,* July 25, 1933.

205. Ibid., July 23, 1933.

206. Mohler, *Wiley Post,* 65.

207. *New York Times,* July 21, 1933.

208. Mohler, *Wiley Post,* 65.

209. *New York Times,* July 23, 1933.

210. Mohler, *Wiley Post,* 65.

211. *New York Times,* July 23, 1933.

212. Mohler, *Wiley Post,* 65.

213. *New York Times,* July 24, 1933.

214. Ibid., July 23, 1933.

215. Ibid., July 24, 1933.

216. Ibid., July 27, 1933.

217. *New York Times,* July 30, 1933.

218. Ibid.

219. Reba Collins, *Will Rogers and Wiley Post in Alaska* (Claremore, Oklahoma: Will Rogers Heritage Press, 1984).

220. Mohler, *Wiley Post,* 72.

221. Ibid.

222. Ibid.

223. Ibid., 74.

224. Ibid. 80.

225. Ibid., 81.

226. Ibid., 83.

227. Ibid., 93.

228. Ibid., 94.

229. *New York Times,* December 4, 1934.

230. Ibid.

231. Ibid., December 8, 1934.

232. *New York Times,* February 23, 1935.

233. Collins, *Will Rogers.*

234. *New York Times,* March 6, 1935.

235. Donald Day, *The Autobiography of Will Rogers* (New York: Houghton Mifflin Co., 1949), 383.

236. Mohler, 107.

237. *New York Times,* June 30, 1935.

238. *The Daily Oklahoman,* August 17, 1935.

239. Day, *The Autobiography of Will Rogers,* 372.

240. Ibid., 392.

241. Ibid., 394.

242. Collins, *Will Rogers,* 4.

243. Ibid.

244. Ibid., 8.

245. Ibid.

246. Ibid., 5.

247. *The Daily Oklahoman,* August 17, 1935.

248. Henry W. Greist, *The Northern Star,* an irregular mimeographed newspaper printed by the doctor who ran the Presbyterian mission hospital at Point Barrow.

249. Associated Press story of August 17, 1935, distributed to the world's newspapers.

250. Ibid.

251. Greist, *The Northern Star.*

252. *New York Times,* August 17, 1935.

253. Ibid.

254. Ibid.

255. Ibid.

256. *The Daily Oklahoman,* August 17, 1935.

257. *New York Times,* August 18, 1935.

258. Ibid.

259. Ibid.

260. From a survey of newspaper clippings from Collins, *Will Rogers.*

261. Ibid.

262. *The Daily Oklahoman,* August 21, 1935.

263. Ibid.

264. Ibid., August 22, 1935.

265. Ibid.

266. Ibid.

267. Ibid.

268. Ibid.

269. Ibid.

270. Ibid.

271. Ibid., August 23, 1935.

272. Ibid.

273. Ibid.

274. Ibid.

275. Mohler, *Wiley Post,* 118.

276. *The Daily Oklahoman,* August 24, 1935.

277. Mohler, *Wiley Post,* 119.

278. *The Daily Oklahoman,* September 26, 1961.

279. Mohler, *Wiley Post,* 12.

COLLECTIONS

F .C. Hall Collection, Oklahoma Heritage Association, Oklahoma City, Oklahoma. Scrapbooks of personal correspondence from the estate of the late F. C. Hall.

NEWSPAPER ARCHIVES

Oklahoma Historical Society, Oklahoma City, Oklahoma. The most complete collection of newspapers printed in Oklahoma.

PUBLISHED MATERIAL

Brown, William R. *Imagemaker: Will Rogers and the American Dream.* Colombia: University of Missouri Press, 1990.

Collins, Reba Neighbors. *Will Rogers and Wiley Post in Alaska.* Claremore, Oklahoma: Will Rogers Heritage Press, 1984.

Day, Donald. *The Autobiography of Will Rogers.* Boston: Houghton Mifflin Co., 1949.

_____. *Will Rogers, A Biography.* New York: David McKay and Co., 1962.

Faulk, Odie B. *Jennys to Jets.* Muskogee, Oklahoma: Western Heritage Books, 1983.

Keith, Harold. *Will Rogers A Boy's Life.* New York: Thomas Crowell Company, 1937.

Mohler, Stanley and Bobby Johnson. *Wiley Post, His Winnie Mae, and the World's First Pressure Suit.* Washington, D.C.: Smithsonian Institution Press, 1971.

O'Brien, P.J. *Will Rogers, Ambassador of Good Will.* Philadelphia: John C. Winston Company, 1935.

Post, Wiley and Harold Gatty. *Around the World in Eight Days.* New York: Garden City Publishing Company, 1931.

Sterling, Bryan and Frances Sterling. *Will Rogers and Wiley Post: Death at Barrow.* New York: M. Evans and Company, 1993.

Wallis, Michael. *Oil Man, the Story of Frank Phillips.* New York: St. Martin's Griffin, 1995.